Richard Quick

WEB DESIGN

4th Edition
All New Content

In Easy Steps is an imprint of Computer Step
Southfield Road · Southam
Warwickshire CV47 0FB · United Kingdom
www.ineasysteps.com

Fourth Edition

Notice of liability
Every effort has been made to ensure this book contains accurate and current information. However, Computer Step and the author shall not be liable for any loss or damage suffered by readers as a result of any information contained herein.

Trademarks
All trademarks are acknowledged as belonging to their respective companies.

Thanks
I'd like to thank the following people for their help, advice and support, both while I was writing the book and before: Lyndon Antcliff, Joe Balestrino, Joern Bargmann, Paul Boag, Chris Campbell, Andy Clarke, Jeff Crowe, William Drummond, Andrei Herasimchuk, Peter Hurley, Roger Johansson, Harshad Kotecha, Pete Lumley, Melanie McFadyean, Anna McKane, Cameron Moll, Joe Pelosi, Marc Pinter-Krainer, Nick Price, Jason Santa Maria, Paul Stanton, Ben Tupper, Paula Turner, Wiebke von Ahn, Ludwig Wendzich and everyone in the web design community.

Special thanks to Dani, Buffy and Hammy (for putting up with the late nights), Mum and Dad (for proofreading and everything else) and Chloe and Peter (who I miss).

Cover Photograph © David Allan Brandt/Stone/Getty Images

Printed and bound in the United Kingdom

ISBN-13 978-1-84078-314-8
ISBN-10 1-84078-314-1

Contents

5 The rules of good design

55

6 Adding pictures

79

7 Links and navigation

93

1 Web design 101

Before you start designing your website, there are a few things you need to know. In this chapter, we give you an overview of the Web and introduce some key online technologies.

World War 3
and the birth of the Internet

The Web has had an explosive impact since it came to the world's attention in the mid 1990s. But the Internet can trace its roots back to an even more explosive invention–the atomic bomb.

When the cold war was in its infancy, the American military realized its normal communication technologies, like telephones, were vulnerable to a nuclear attack by the Soviets.

When you make a phone call you are connected to a central exchange, which then connects you to the phone you are calling. The problem is that if the exchange stops working (say it is blown up) then you can't make any calls.

So, at the height of the Cold War the US military developed a network of computers that would carry on communicating with each other even after a nuclear attack. They called it *ARPAnet*.

Like any great invention, the idea behind ARPAnet was beautifully simple. Rather than connecting through a central exchange, each of the computers was able to directly communicate with other computers on the network.

When one computer needed to send a message to another, it would break that message down into smaller chunks, called *packets*. These packets would then find their own way through the network until they reached their destination.

Hot tip

There's lots more information about the Internet, the World Wide Web and email in our book **Internet in easy steps**.

Over the years ARPANET grew into a worldwide network of interconnected computers which became known as the *Internet*.

Along came a spider

From its birth in the 1960s until the 1990s, the Internet steadily grew in popularity, becoming an academic tool as much as a military one. However, it wasn't until the creation of the *World Wide Web* (or just the *Web* for short) that the Internet crossed over from being a tool of a technically gifted few, to part of everyday mainstream life.

The Web, as well as *HTML* (the language web pages are written in), was invented by Tim Berners-Lee, a British physicist working at the CERN particle physics laboratory in Geneva, Switzerland.

Berners-Lee hit upon the idea of using *hypertext* documents across the Internet so that scientists, like himself, could share information no matter where they were in the world.

The idea of hypertext had been around for some time. Hypertext is electronic text with links to further information – similar to cross-references in a dictionary or references in an academic paper.

Berners-Lee's brilliant idea was to combine the idea of hypertext with the worldwide computer network we call the Internet. Of course, there are several very clever technical innovations underlying the Web, but at its heart the original idea was just to provide a way for physicists in Europe to share information easily with their counterparts around the globe.

This simple and refreshingly altruistic idea – of using the Internet to share information through hypertext documents – is the basis of the Web we know and depend upon today.

The rest is history. In just 10 years, the Web went from being the brainchild of an English physicist to a force that could shape and break the global economy.

Today, over a billion people are thought to be online – one sixth of the world's population.

AAA 398
AUGUST 6, 1945

What is HTML?

HTML is the language websites are written in. The letters stand for *HyperText Markup Language*. It might sound complicated, but it's actually pretty easy to understand. Here's an example of some HTML code:

```
Web Design in easy steps is a great book.
```

Yes, it's that simple. A web page written in HTML doesn't need to contain any more than a few lines of text.

Is that it?

Not quite. A web page which contained nothing but plain text would look a bit boring, but you can make it look more exciting using bits of HTML code called *tags*. Here's a slightly more complicated piece of HTML:

```
<img src="/images/cover.jpg" alt="Book cover" />

<p>Other books in the <b>In Easy Steps</b>
series include <i>Photoshop Elements 6 in easy
steps</i> and <i>HTML in easy steps</i>.</p>
```

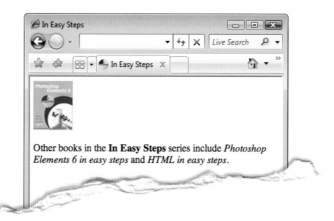

This time the text is enhanced, or *marked up,* using some simple HTML tags. The `<i>` tag makes the text italic and the `<b>` tag makes it bold. You've probably also noticed the `</i>` and `</b>` tags – they tell your *web browser* where the italic and bold text should stop. There's also a tag to add an image (`<img … />`) and one for a paragraph (`<p>…</p>`).

As well as tags to make text bold or italic, HTML has tags to change the font, add headings or colors, link to another page or even add sound or movies.

Tag soup

Next time you're on the Web, have a look at the HTML code for your favorite website. To do this in Internet Explorer, just click the right mouse button somewhere on the web page and choose "view source". You'll probably see something like this:

```
<link rel="stylesheet" type="text/css" href="css/master.css" />
<script type="text/javascript" src="js/scripts.js"></script>

</head>

<body>
    <div class="skipper">
        <a href="#content" accesskey="2"><img src="images/spacer.gif" width="1" height="1" alt="skip navigation" /></a>
    </div>
    <div class="wrapper">
        <div class="top-nav">
            <form id="search_form" method="post" action="#">
                <div class="top-nav-search">
                    <label for="search_box" class="hide">Search</label>
                    <input type="text" name="search_box" id="search_box" value="Search" />
                    <input type="image" src="images/button_go.gif" alt="Go" />
                </div>
            </form>
            <div class="top-nav-lnks-holder">
                <ul class="link-list">
                    <li><a href="#" class="lnk-wdth-1 on">home</a></li>
                    <li><a href="#" class="lnk-wdth-2">books</a></li>
                    <li><a href="#" class="lnk-wdth-3">corporate information</a></li>
                    <li><a href="#" class="lnk-wdth-4">resource center</a></li>
                    <li><a href="#" class="lnk-wdth-5">contact us</a></li>
                </ul>
            </div>
        </div>
        <div class="breadcrumb">
            <!-- No breadcrumb on homepage, but keep div for formatting //--><h1 class="hide">Homepage</h1>
        </div>
        <div id="content">

            <div class="col-1">

                <div class="home-main-panel" style="background-image: url(images/books/3d_home/main-panel_00001.jpg);">
                    <h2>Book of the day</h2>
                    <h2>Photoshop Elements 3 takes the editing and organizing of digital images to a new level. <strong>Photoshop Elem
                    <p>Photoshop Elements 3 in easy steps</a>
                    get the most out of this great software. </p>More about Photoshop Elements 3 in easy steps</a>
anyone who wants to   <a href="#" class="chevron-link"><h2>WIN! </h2>Online Poker in easy steps</div></a><img src="ima
            </div>                       class="switch">              center</h2>Downloads articles and more</a></li></div>
```

The HTML for the **www.ineasysteps.com** website

It might look complicated, but remember it's just some text which has been marked up with HTML tags.

I'm scared. Do I need to learn HTML?

No. There are lots of web design programs that write HTML for you, like Dreamweaver (**dreamweaver.com**) or Nvu (**nvu.com**). You simply edit the page, just like you would with a Word document.

You could also get a web programmer (or *web developer*) to do the HTML coding for you after you've designed the site. A lot of professional web designers take this approach.

Of course, if you know HTML, you'll find it a lot easier to put your design ideas into practice. Most professional websites are hand-coded these days, but using a visual tool like Dreamweaver is fine if you're doing a personal site.

However you build your website, it's important to know what HTML is and also to have an idea of how it works.

Hot tip

Believe it or not, HTML can be fun to learn. Why not find out more with our book **HTML in easy steps**?

Create stylish sites with CSS

You can use HTML to control almost every part of the look-and-feel of your website, from the fonts and colors you use, to the position of elements on the page. However, doing everything in HTML isn't easy.

Hot tip

To find out more about CSS, take a look at our book **CSS in easy steps**.

A better way to control the way your website looks is to use *Cascading Style Sheets* (or CSS for short).

The first thing to realize is that you don't use CSS on its own, you use it *with* HTML. You still use HTML tags to mark up your web page, but then you use CSS to control how elements on the page look and where they go. Here's how the HTML from page 10 might look if we styled it with CSS:

```
p {width: 300px; float: left; background-color:
yellow; padding: 10px; margin: 0;}

img {float: right;}
```

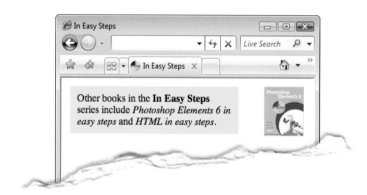

You can create truly stunning sites using the power of CSS.

Black music website Chocolate Magazine uses CSS to achieve an edgy urban look.

A website's CSS is usually stored in a separate file which the individual HTML web pages call in. The advantage of this is that one CSS file can control the look of your entire site. So, if you want to change the color of all the text on your site, you just make one small change in the CSS file and it's done.

Css has quite a few other advantages over just using HTML. Css sites are quicker to download, they get better search engine rankings, they're easier to adapt for mobile phones, PDAs and web TV and they're more accessible to people with disabilities.

Introducing Javascript

So you've created a stunning website with HTML and CSS, but what if you want your pages to react to the way people use them? In that case you'll probably need some *Javascript*.

Javascript is a programming language that you can use to control how your web pages behave, just like CSS controls how they look.

You've probably seen quite a bit of Javascript in action without realizing it while you were surfing the Web.

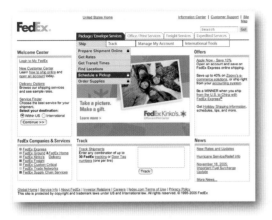

FedEx.com uses Javascript for its drop down menus

The most common use of Javascript is almost certainly to launch those annoying pop-up adverts you see all over the place, but you can also use it to create drop down menus, warn people when they've missed their email address off a form or calculate your mortgage payments for the next 30 years.

Because Javascript can tell which web browser you're using, it's also very useful for fixing bugs in your web page that only show up in certain browsers.

What about DHTML?

Dynamic HTML, or DHTML for short, uses Javascript and CSS to create moving elements on a web page, like drop down menus or annoying little stars that follow your mouse pointer.

It used to be very popular a few years ago, but these days people tend to prefer websites that have interesting content or do something useful, rather than silly gimmicks.

Beware

Javascript isn't the same as Java, although the two languages look quite similar.

Javascript's inventors originally called it Live Script, but renamed it as a marketing ploy when Java became popular.

13

Hot tip

Javascript is a very useful skill for any web designer.

There are lots of websites to help you get started or you could read **Javascript in easy steps**.

The magic of
multimedia

The Web has come a long way since it was used to share physics papers. These days, there's very little you can't do on your site as long as you've got the time, knowledge and imagination.

Plug-ins
By themselves web browsers can only display the pictures and text that make up ordinary web pages. If you want to get them to do anything more cutting-edge, you'll need to install a small program called a *plug-in* that extends your browser's abilities.

They're usually free to download, but it's important to realize that not everyone will have them installed.

Music videos and samples of recent tracks help attract visitors to pop stars' websites like **beyonceonline.com**

Flash
The most popular multimedia plug-in by far is *Adobe Flash*.

It's a powerful technology that allows you to create entire sites with advanced multimedia capabilities.

Flash sites are much more dynamic than ordinary HTML ones. Text and images slide smoothly in and out of view, creating a far more engaging experience for the visitor.

Flash can play audio and video and, can even interact with a database, to allow you to create web-based applications that are as quick and easy to use as programs on your PC.

It's not all good news though. Flash sites can be slow to download and often hard to use, as they've been designed to look good in someone's portfolio, rather than with the end user in mind. Flash sites are also less accessible to people with disabilities than normal sites.

Streaming video

Let's face it, many people would rather watch the film of a book than read the book itself. Until connection speeds get a lot faster, video isn't going to take over from ordinary web pages, but it's a great way to make your site stand out from the crowd.

There are several popular online video formats, including *Real Player*, *Windows Media Player* and *Quicktime*. Windows Media Player comes pre-installed on most PCs and Quicktime comes with all Apple Macs. Most sites with video usually offer it in at least two of these formats, with a higher-quality version for people with broadband and a faster-downloading version for people who are still using a modem.

As well as video, Quicktime VR can also produce virtual 3D views of objects and landscapes.

The virtual tour on **sydneyoperahouse.com** lets people explore the building and see 360° views of Sydney harbor.

The designers used Flash and Quicktime VR to create a distinctive and easy to use tour.

15

Radio shows can be downloaded as MP3s on **bbc.co.uk**

Audio

Sound and music are often forgotten on the Web, which gives you a great opportunity to make your site memorable.

Audio files can either be embedded in a web page or, more commonly, are downloaded by people visiting your site.

This map of the Boxing Day Tsunami shows multimedia can be used for education as well as entertainment.

Shockwave

Shockwave is produced by Adobe, the company behind Flash, and it's got a lot in common with its more popular cousin.

Shockwave can produce 3D graphics which are almost as good as those on a Playstation and it's often used to produce online games.

Domain names & servers

Nobody knows exactly how many websites there are on the Internet, but it could be as many as 100 million. With so many sites, how will anyone find yours? The easiest way is for them to type your *domain name* into their web browser.

Here are a few domain names you probably already know:

- **amazon.com**
- **google.com**
- **hotmail.com**
- **bbc.co.uk**
- **ebay.com**

Domain names are like the phone numbers of the Web. It's a unique name given to your site and ends in a short extension like **.com**, **.net** or **.co.uk**

You can buy domain names for a few dollars these days and the registration period lasts for between one and ten years, depending on how much you pay.

Most of the great domain names have been taken already, but it's always possible to come up with something memorable. Make sure your name's easy to spell and doesn't sound like another word, **bookcellar.com** could easily be confused with **bookseller.com**

Servers

People across the globe use the Web at all hours of the day and night. So, if they're going to be able to see your website you'll need to host it on a suitable computer that's permanently connected to the Internet, known as a *server*.

Hot tip

For more information on choosing a web host, turn to page 160.

You could set up a server in your bedroom, but it's cheaper, easier and more reliable to get a web hosting company to host your site on a professional server.

Prices start from a few dollars a year, going up to several thousand dollars a month for top of the line web hosting. You'll need to pay more if your site gets lots of visitors.

As well as your site, most hosting companies will host your email accounts as well, allowing you to set up your own personalized email addresses (*me@mycompany.com*).

Many will also allow you to run programming languages like PHP or ASP and set up a database.

If you're on a very small budget there are even sites that offer free hosting in return for putting adverts on your site (like **tripod.com** or **geocities.com**).

Database-driven websites

Think of a website you visit often and the chances are you use it to *do* something. You might buy books online, send email, download music or take part in an online auction.

Any site that does more than display a few pages of text and pictures, will need some kind of *server-side program* or *database*.

Hot tip

Online shops, like Barnes & Noble's, store information in a database including orders, book prices and descriptions.

Popular web databases include:

- MySQL
- Access
- SQL server
- Oracle

Web programming languages and databases
You've probably heard of at least one web programming language. Some of the most common include *Java*, *ASP* and *PHP*. These are often called server-side languages as they run on your web server, rather than the computer of someone visiting your site.

Most web programs store information in a database, like *MySQL* or *Oracle*, and then use it to create HTML web pages on demand.

For example, an online shop will store each product's name, description, price, code and photo in a database. When you click on a link to a product, the programming language looks in the database and creates a web page to display all the information.

Which one should I use?
Each programming language and database has its own strengths and weaknesses. PHP is very easy to learn and quick to program, while Java is very efficient and secure. MySQL databases are free and easy to set up while Oracle can handle hundreds of thousands of visitors, but is very expensive.

In most cases, the programmer usually chooses the language and database that they know best.

Hot tip

Lots of sites use PHP and MySQL as they're both free and easy to use.

PHP 5 in easy steps and **SQL in easy steps** are great places to start if you need a database-driven website.

Should I hire a web designer?

This might seem like a strange question. Surely you bought this book because you wanted to design your site yourself, right?

Well, creating a website is a complicated process—here are some of the things you might have to do:

- Planning, strategy and information architecture
- Graphic design
- Copy writing
- HTML, CSS and Javascript coding
- Server-side programming and database development

In a large company, each of these would be a full-time job and not many people can do all of them well. You might find you're really good at design, but not so good with databases. Or you might find you enjoy doing HTML, but not copy writing. In that case, it's worth thinking about paying someone to help you out.

Where do I find a web designer or developer?
Start off by searching Google for web designers or programmers in your local area or try the Yellow Pages. It's often best to be able to meet the designer face to face to talk through your ideas.

You can employ a freelance web designer, a larger web design company or an advertising agency. A freelancer will normally be cheaper, but an agency may have more resources. You could also consider advertising for a freelance or full-time web designer on sites like **authenticjobs.com** and **freelancers.net**

How do I choose someone?
Anyone can be a web designer or developer, you don't need a degree or professional accreditation. That means there's lots of competition—but it also means there are a lot of cowboys.

The first thing to look at is the work your web designer has done before. If you like their style that's a very good sign. If you're impressed with what you see, ask how much they charge.

Finally, ask if you can contact some of their past clients to check they were happy with the work and the service. Your relationship with your web designer is as important as the quality of their work. Successful websites are developed over time, so look for a designer you can build an ongoing relationship with.

Hot tip

It's easy to tell if you like a web designer's style, but it's also important to make sure their sites are up to scratch technically.

Ask them if they use web standards (see page 153) and check if their sites have any mistakes in the HTML code using this site: **http://validator.w3.org**

2 Planning your website

If you built a bridge without a blueprint, it would probably fall down. A website that hasn't been planned is just as likely to fail. This chapter will take you through some of the steps you need to take in order to ensure your site is a success.

Setting a goal for your site

Most websites fail. For every Google or Amazon there are thousands of sites that don't make it, so what can you do to make your website a success?

The first thing you need to do to avoid failure is to define exactly what you mean by success. What do you want your website to achieve?

Before you do anything you should decide on a short, clear goal for your site and then write it down. Possible goals include:

- To make enough money selling your line of hand-made jewelry to give up your day job
- To tell everyone how great your pet hamster is
- To sell your range of skateboards to people outside California
- To get more parents to send their children to your school
- To fill more rooms in your hotel during the off-season
- To educate divers about the dangers they pose to coral reefs
- To raise money for cancer research
- To help people understand trigonometry

It's important that you only set one goal for your site. If you try to do too many things at once, you'll fail.

Focus on achieving your goal

Your goal can help you make the right decisions when designing your website – but only if you keep focused on it.

Whenever you need to make a decision, ask yourself which of the options is most likely to help you achieve your goal.

One decision you must take for any site is how large to make the text. Small text often looks nicer, but larger text is more readable.

Imagine you were designing a site for a financial advisor whose goal was "to get new customers". Would large or small text help you to achieve the goal better? Larger text would be better, as most investors are older people and many wear glasses.

But what if their goal was "to get more *young* customers"? Smaller text might be more likely to appeal to younger investors, although you still need to make sure they can read it.

Hot tip

Your goal needs to be clear, so you can test whether you've achieved it or not.

If your aim is something vague, like "to make a good site", then it'll be hard to tell if you have succeeded or failed.

Beware

When more than one person is working on a site, they may have their own personal goals.

Designers may be more interested in creating an attractive website for their portfolio than a site that makes money.

Having a goal written down helps make sure everyone is pulling in the same direction.

Understanding your visitors

A website without visitors is as pointless as a pencil without lead. To make sure the people who visit your site don't leave straight away you'll need to identify your *target audience*, the people you *want* to visit your site, so you can ensure the design and content will appeal to them.

You need to know as much about your target audience as possible. Ask yourself lots of questions about them:

- How old are they?
- What kind of jobs do they have?
- Where do they live?
- What computer do they own?
- How much do they use the Web?
- What other sites do they visit?
- Why have they come to your site?

The call to action

Once you've got a clear idea of who your target audience is, you'll need to think about how you are going to use this knowledge to achieve the goal you've set for your site.

If you're planning a business site then you probably want the visitor to buy something from you, either now or in the future. If your site is non-commercial, you probably still want your visitor to *do* something specific, like donate money to a charity or improve their knitting.

So, how do you get your visitors to do what you want? Well, you need to ask them – and it needs to be obvious. There's no point in having a "buy now" button if your visitor doesn't notice it.

Your whole site, from the design to the writing, should be focused on getting your visitors to take up your *call to action*. For some sites, like Amazon, the action they want the visitor to perform might be to make an online purchase, but for others it could simply be tempting the visitor to make a phone call or send an email.

Whatever your call to action is, you'll need to understand your target audience in order to get them to perform it.

Don't forget

Nobody knows more about your target audience than your customers themselves.

Find some potential customers and ask them what they like, what they do for a living, and what they'd want out of a website like yours.

Check out the competition

There's no such thing as an original idea any more, at least not on the Web. If you're designing a new site it's almost certain that somebody somewhere will have done something similar before.

You might not welcome this competition but try to think of it as free market research. Your competitors may have spent a lot of time and money coming up with ideas for their site and there's nothing to stop you using those ideas for free. Take a look at your competitors' websites to see what they've done well and what they've done badly.

Learn from other people's mistakes

If you're able to offer visitors something your competitors don't, there's a good chance they'll start using your site instead.

Visit other people's sites and think like an awkward customer. What's wrong with their site? What could they do better? What are they missing?

Here are some of the things you might find:

- Their site looks cheap so I don't trust them. A site that looks professional would make me much more likely to buy online
- I don't have Flash, so I can't use their site
- It takes me too long to find the books I want
- There are lots of spelling mistakes on the site and I found the articles boring, even though it's about my favorite singer
- The site takes a long time to load, I can't wait that long so I'll probably go to another site instead
- I found the order forms really confusing. I'd rather call them up than buy from their website

Credit where credit's due

It's probably easy to pick holes in your competition's website, but also remember to focus on the things they've done well.

Imagine you're a potential customer coming to the site. Try to perform one of the "tasks" you'd want them to carry out, such as finding the company's phone number and address or buying something online.

How easy is it to carry out the tasks? How long did it take? What impression of the company did you get?

Beware

Looking at other people's websites for inspiration is a great idea. Copying them isn't.

It may be tempting to cut corners by copying the terms and conditions from another site, but it's also against the law.

When Google launched in 1999, there were already dozens of highly-successful search engines.

However, in just a few years it became the number one. Why? It was quicker, searched more web pages and gave better results than the others.

22

What to include on your site

The biggest mistake you can make when creating your website is not to focus on your goal. The second biggest mistake is to focus too hard on it.

Remember, your site isn't aimed at you, it's aimed at your visitors. So you should think about what *they* want from your site. Ask yourself why they would visit your website. What's in it for *them*?

If you run a surfwear company, your primary motivation for having a site will be to make money by selling your line of wetsuits and surfwear. However, it's highly unlikely anybody visiting your site will care whether or not you make any money.

They might be interested in buying a top of the line wetsuit, but they might just as well want to find out more about surfing or look at girls in bikinis.

Imagine yourself as a potential visitor—what would *you* want from a website? Make a list of all the things your target audience would search Google for. If you sell surfwear you might find people search for "surf lessons", "weather forecast California" or surfing legend "Kelly Slater".

Rather than just having an online shop, why not create a monthly magazine with contents that your target audience will want to read? Our imaginary surf shop might have tips for beginners, interviews with pro surfers and reviews of local surfing beaches.

Not only are people more likely to find you if your content is relevant to them, they're also more likely to link to you from their blog and tell their friends about you.

Don't lose sight of your own goals though. If you want to sell your products online, remind your visitors about your shop while they're reading your articles.

Hot tip

If you're not sure what your visitors might want from your site, ask them.

Before you launch, put up an online questionnaire and offer people who complete it the chance of winning one of your products.

Then run a short Google AdWords campaign (see page 175) to get people to visit your site and questionnaire.

The 3 click rule

People can be very impatient online. Make them wait too long and they'll be off quicker than you can blink. So it's vital that your visitors can complete whatever task they came to your site to carry out as quickly as possible.

Ideally, you should design your site so your visitors can complete any major task, such as buying a book or finding your helpline number, without having to click on more than three links.

This is called the *three click rule* and it's one of the best-known principles of web design.

For example, if you want to use Google to find a dental surgery in Atlanta you would:

- Type "dental surgery Atlanta" into the search box and then click on the "Google search" button – that's one click
- Then, you'd search through the results on the first page, choose one and then click on the link – that's two clicks

So, within just two clicks of the Google homepage, you can find a dentist in Atlanta, which is the task you wanted to carry out.

What do *you* want people to do on your site?

Ask yourself what the major tasks are, that you want people to complete, when they come to your site.

If your site has an online DVD shop, you'll want people to be able to find the DVD they want and choose to buy it, within three clicks. If it takes a few clicks more for them to fill in their credit card details, that doesn't matter.

Likewise, if you give guitar lessons, you'll want people to be able to find your hourly rate and then contact you within three clicks.

It takes just 3 clicks from the **bn.com** homepage to find a Photoshop book and choose to buy it.

Point them in the right direction

Remember, the reason someone comes to your site may not be the same as the reason you want them there. People often visit *real* shops to browse. Likewise, people visit an online shop to look up some trivia (Who plays the bad guy from *Die Hard*?) or find out a release date (When's the new *Harry Potter* out on DVD?).

However, just because your visitor didn't come to the site to buy something doesn't mean they must leave empty handed. It's your job as the web designer to tempt them into making a purchase.

4 types of web page

Homepage

Your homepage is the first page of your site. You can think of it as a cover and a contents page rolled into one.

A lot of designers make the mistake of trying to fit too much into the homepage, thinking this will make the site look full of useful information. In fact, long lists of links are more likely to scare visitors away.

One simple message on your homepage, with a few links to other sections of the site, will often be more inviting for users. If you do need to cover lots on the homepage, try to divide the page into several sections with one obvious "main" section.

www.ineasysteps.com contains all four of the most common types of web page.

Transitional page

A transitional page is one that only exists to give people a choice of which page to look at next. These pages should be simple and quick to load as visitors are only interested in the *next* page, not the transitional page itself.

Try to give your visitors fewer than seven main links to choose from. This will speed things up for them.

Content page

Content pages are there to be read. They're often longer than other pages. It's important that these pages are easy to read, so make the contrast between the background and text strong enough and use a large readable font.

Remember these pages are also the most likely to be printed, so test how they look on your printer.

Action page

Some pages on your site will require your visitors to take some kind of action, such as filling in a contact form or giving their credit card details.

It's important that these pages are easy to use, as visitors will often leave the site if they find forms too long or confusing. If you need to gather lots of information, split the form into clearly defined sections. This will make things more manageable for the visitor.

Creating a sitemap

A sitemap is a visual plan of your website showing the pages and how they link to each other. In other words, a map of your site.

If your site is small you'll have a simple sitemap (like the one shown here), but the larger it becomes, the more important it is to have a logical, well thought out sitemap so your visitors don't get lost or confused.

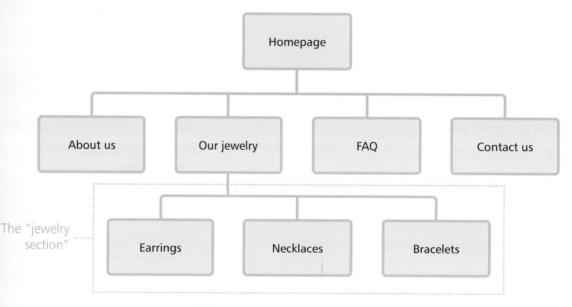

The "jewelry section"

A tidy site is an easy to use site

When you visit your local supermarket, you'll find similar products close to each other. All the fruit and vegetables, for example, are in one place. Why? Because it's easier for you to find what you want, especially if you haven't visited the store before.

It should be the same with your site. If your pages are randomly scattered through the website nobody will be able to find them. When planning your site make sure it's organized in a clear, easy to understand way with related pages grouped into sections.

Think like a customer, not an employee

Don't make the mistake of using the structure of your company as the basis for your website's structure. It might make sense for you to keep Sony and Panasonic products separate in your warehouse, but a customer will want to buy a TV or a DVD player, not "something that's made by Panasonic". Split your site into sections that make sense to the visitor.

Hot tip

Don't have any more than seven pages in a section if you can help it.

Experts have found that people find more than seven choices confusing.

Try condensing 2 pages into 1 or splitting the pages into two sections.

The essential information

Contact information

One of the main reasons people will visit your website is to look up your phone number. Make it easy for them with a prominent link to your contact details on your homepage.

Make sure to include your postal address, phone and fax numbers, as not everyone wants to use email. It may even be worth putting your contact details on every page of the site. After all, you wouldn't want to lose an order because a potential customer couldn't find your phone number, would you?

Not everyone will be able to send you an email there and then (they may be at work) so it's a good idea to add a contact form as well. These are very easy to set up.

Beware

Some people get scared to put their contact details on their site in case too many people call them. Don't be.

Having too many customers is a problem most business people would kill for.

Contact pages often look boring, but they don't have to, as this site shows

Frequently asked questions

Websites are great at generating new business, but they can also save you time and money when dealing with existing customers.

A well written FAQ page on your site can save you valuable time answering phone calls or emails.

Draw up a list of the most common questions you get asked and put answers to them online. If you've got staff who regularly speak to customers, like your receptionist or sales people, ask them what questions they get asked most.

Make sure your visitors know you've got an FAQ page on your site, by adding a prominent link, or there's no point in having it.

Planning your look-and-feel

You might not think the way your site looks is very important—but you'd be wrong. People's first impressions will affect their opinion of the site and your business.

In fact, it takes less than a 20th of a second for people to form a lasting opinion of a website.

Before you start work on the actual design of the site, you should have a clear idea of what *message* you want your design to communicate and what *style* of design you intend to use.

First, think about the impression you want your target audience to be left with when they visit your site. Should they think of you as "trustworthy", "young" or "high-tech"?

Then look at other people's sites, as well as ads in magazines and newspapers, to find a style you think would work for you. Once you find a style you like, ask a few potential customers what they think. After all, they're the people who'll be using your site.

Mood boards

An effective way to plan your site's look-and-feel is to create a *mood board*.

Find objects with a style, color or shape which reflect how you want the site to look, for example magazine ads and pieces of fabric, and then stick them to a sheet of card.

This will help you establish a *mood* for the site when you're designing it, such as "dark and gothic" or "young and funky".

A mood board for a 1970s inspired website*

A mood board will give you a good starting point for your site's design and can help communicate your ideas to other people. It should also give you ideas for colors, images and typefaces.

Beware

Don't be scared of looking different from your competition.

Just because every other financial advisor's website is navy blue doesn't mean yours should be.

28

*Thanks to Andy Clarke of **stuffandnonsense.co.uk** for the mood board.

7 steps to a great site

Planning

Before you start work on your website you need to plan it thoroughly. Make sure you set a clear goal for your site and then use your knowledge of your target audience to work out how you are going to achieve it.

Design

The next stage is to design your site in a graphics package, like Photoshop. It's important to finalize the design before you start to build the site, as it's much quicker and cheaper to make changes in Photoshop than it is in HTML.

Writing and content gathering

During the planning stage, you should have decided which pages your site will contain. Now it's time to write the text and decide which pictures to use. You can often create the content at the same time as the site's being designed.

Building the site

Once you know what the site's going to look like and what it will contain, you need to turn it into an actual website. You'll use HTML and CSS to create web pages based on your Photoshop designs. You might create a database as well.

Testing

Does the site work? Can people use it as you'd expected? Before launching your site you need to test it thoroughly. Check for broken links and make sure the site works on different browsers. Also, check for spelling mistakes.

Promotion

Your site's completed so now you can sit back and watch the cash roll in—right? Not quite. Getting your website up there is just the start; now you need to get people to visit, using search engines, marketing and word of mouth.

Evolution

Once your site's finished and visitors start arriving, you may think your work's done—but it isn't. The best sites constantly make small improvements and test new ideas.

Hot tip

Changing the design of your site after you've coded the HTML and developed the database can be time consuming, costly and frustrating.

To ensure you don't make this mistake, get everyone involved to sign a document after each step, confirming it has been successfully completed.

Once a step has been *signed off* it's important you don't make any further changes.

Know what you're aiming for

One of the most common reasons sites fail, is that the owners and designers never set any clear goals for the site to begin with.

There are lots of great sites on the Web, but not all of them would be appropriate for you. Nobody could reasonably claim Google wasn't a successful site, but would you want a similar design for the new Nike website? Probably not.

If you've got a clear goal, the web designer–whether it's you or someone else–can gear your site towards achieving that goal.

1 Using standard navigation and search should make the site easier to use.

2 A well-promoted contest should help increase casual traffic and bring people back to the site regularly.

3 Grouping several sections from the old site into a new "resource center" should make things easier for visitors.

4 The old site organized books in alphabetical order. We thought visitors would be more likely to want to explore the books by subject area.

Our main goal with **ineasysteps.com** was to create a site that gave a more accurate impression of the company and strengthened the branding. We also had two secondary goals:

- To make the site more accessible and search engine friendly using modern XHTML and CSS coding techniques
- To increase casual traffic to the site

The main target audience was book industry professionals, but we also wanted to appeal to *In Easy Steps* readers, as well as casual Internet users, who might find the site through search engines.

As well as a thorough redesign, we reorganized the content so that it made more sense to *In Easy Steps* readers. We also added several sections to increase our search engine visibility, including a database of articles by our team of authors and an online store selling e-books of out-of-print titles.

3 Anatomy of a web page

Before you design a house, you need to know what houses are made of: walls, doors, windows, floors and roofs. Before you design your website, you'll need to understand what elements you can use in your design.

Body copy

Most websites have lots of words on them. They're used for navigation, in logos and as headlines. *Body copy* is the name web designers give to the words that form the content of the web page, such as a news story or product description.

Content is king

In many websites the content is the most important aspect of the site by far. Although it's important that a news website, like CNN or the BBC, looks attractive and is easy to use: people come to the site to read the articles. If they're not up to scratch, the site will struggle to attract visitors back.

1 This web page from **newyorkmetro.com** has lots of different elements on it, like navigation and adverts.

However, the body copy—a story about actress Julianne Moore, highlighted in green—is the only reason the page exists. Without it, this page would be pointless.

Can you read it?

If people come to your site for the articles or product descriptions, it's important they can read the copy easily. Use a reasonable size font on a plain white or light-colored background. This will also make your pages easier to print.

Headings

Headings help your visitors scan a web page to see if they want to read the body copy. They split the content into manageable sections and can be used by blind people using *screen readers** to navigate the web page. Headings, if used correctly, also help search engines to index your web pages.

How HTML handles headings

In a printed document, like a newspaper or brochure, you can use headings wherever you feel like it. However, because web pages are written using HTML you have to use them in a certain way.

HTML has six levels of heading. The main page heading uses an ⟨h1⟩ tag and should be near the top of the page. There are then six levels of sub-heading, ranging from ⟨h2⟩ to ⟨h6⟩.

Remember, headings are used to help the reader scan the page. Each sub-heading should break the page down into smaller sections of information.

If your page is on "Traveling around Europe", that should be your main heading (⟨h1⟩). You could then have ⟨h2⟩ sub-headings on Great Britain, France, Germany and so on. Under Great Britain you might have ⟨h3⟩ sub-headings on England, Wales, Scotland and Northern Ireland.

Each time you're breaking the page into smaller, more specific sections. So, if your visitors wanted to visit Wales, they could skip straight to the right section, without having to read all about traveling in France.

1 A well-coded web page should have one (and only one) main heading, which is coded using an ⟨h1⟩ tag in HTML.

The main heading should sum up the contents of the page, helping the visitor to decide whether or not to read the rest of it.

2 Sub-headings help the visitor get straight to the information they want, without having to read the whole page.

*See page 155 for more info on screen readers.

Hyperlinks

Hyperlinks (or *links* for short) are words or images which take you to another page (or another part of the same page) when you click on them.

Links in body copy are usually underlined and in a different color from the surrounding text, so visitors realize they are links. They often change color when you hold your mouse pointer over them.

1 Links are normally underlined and a different color from the rest of the body copy, which helps visitors recognize them as links.

Why be different?

It's often tempting to try to make your website different from others just for the sake of it. One way a lot of web designers try to be different is by removing the underline from links. This is easy to do with css and sometimes it might be appropriate–but, before you do it, ask yourself one question. Why?

There's certainly nothing wrong with trying to be original. Remember that your visitors will be familiar with underlined text representing links, though. If you change it, you'll confuse some of them, so make sure you have a good reason for doing so.

Images

There aren't many websites these days, especially commercial ones, that don't use images.

In fact, there are probably a lot more images on a typical website than you might think. Because HTML was originally only designed to share academic papers, anything more complicated than simple text or a web form has to use an image. Every curve, icon, logo, gradient or pattern is actually an image. Some web designers will even use images instead of text for headings, as it gives them greater control over the fonts and positioning.

Images are used throughout the Winter Olympics site to control the pages' look-and-feel.

Even some "text" is really an image, as the designer can specify exactly which font is used.

The Winter Olympics site (above) has some obvious images, like the photo of the skier, the logo and cartoons in the right-hand column. However, the red and orange pattern at the top of the page, the colored curves in the right-hand column and even the "passion lives here" text are actually images.

Tiled images

Background images in a web page can be *tiled* (or repeated) horizontally, vertically or in both directions.

The gradient on Winter Olympics site's gray navigation bar was created by repeating a narrow image horizontally.

Lists

You've probably seen or used lists in Word documents many times, either bullet points or numbered lists.

There are three types of list in HTML:

- Unordered lists (bullet points)
- Ordered lists (numbered lists)
- Definition lists (used to define words or phrases–for example, in a dictionary)

Lists are useful for grouping pieces of information together visually. If the pieces of information are in no particular order, say a list of good websites, then you would use an unordered list. However, if the list was of the top ten pop singles sold, then you'd use a numbered (or ordered) list.

Definition lists aren't used as much as the other two types of list, although they may be useful if your site has a glossary.

1 Ineasysteps.com uses an unordered list for the sitemap.

Notice that some sections are indented. This is done by having *nestled lists* (lists within a list).

2 Perhaps surprisingly, the site navigation is also a list of links that has been styled with css to look totally different.

Hidden lists

Because lists are used to group together related pieces of information, it makes logical sense to group related information or links into a list. However, visually you might not always want a group of information to have bullet points.

This is where the power of css is useful. Just because something appears in the HTML as a list, it doesn't need to look like a set of bullet points. You can use css to style a list to look any way you want. For example, the navigation on ineasysteps.com is actually just a list of links that has been styled with css to look a certain way.

Tables

Tables are used to present complex information in an easy to understand way. They're especially useful for numerical information. In print, you often find tables in the business sections of newspapers or in scientific or engineering reports.

Tables can also be used in web pages, wherever you've got rows and columns of data. Financial information is particularly well suited to being presented as a table, but simpler lists of information, like names and addresses, can also use them.

 Barnes & Noble's corporate website uses tables to display financial information, like stock prices.

Using tables for layout

A few years ago, most web pages used tables to control the positioning of elements on the web page. The reason people did this was that at the time it was the only way to reliably lay out a web page.

Although many sites still use tables for layout, it's better, for a number of reasons, to use css for layout and just use tables to format data.

Hot tip

A List Apart, a popular web design magazine, has some great articles on the best way to use and code tables.

Visit: **alistapart.com**

Forms

Online forms are very similar to the type of printed forms you have to fill out when you apply for a new credit card or mortgage.

When you find a form on a web page, you fill in the *fields* (blank boxes) and click on a *submit button*, which usually says something like "Submit", "Send" or "Go".

There are several different types of field a form can use. The most common are simple text boxes where you might fill in your name, address or email. There are also *check boxes*, *select boxes* (also called *drop downs*), *text areas* and *radio buttons*.

1   Visitors can usually type anything into *text boxes*.

2   *Text areas* are similar to text boxes but can contain many lines of text.

3   *Radio buttons* give the user a choice between two or more possibilities.

4   *Check boxes* can be ticked or unticked.

5   Clicking on the *submit button* sends the form.

What happens when you push the button?

When you submit a form, Internet Explorer sends the information you've entered to a program on the server. The program (usually written in a language like PHP or ASP) will then take that information and *do* something with it.

For example, when you submit a contact form, the program might send the site's owner an email with your name, telephone number and message, or it might add all your information to a database.

Checking the data

Often a form will have fields where only certain types of entries are acceptable. For instance, *"info@richardquickdesign.com"* is a valid email address but "0123456789" isn't.

In that case, you can check (or *validate*) the form to ensure the visitor has filled in all the fields correctly. This can either be done before the form is submitted (using Javascript) or afterwards.

Header & footer

A header is an area at the top of a web page which is reused on several pages across a website. Similarly, a footer is an area at the bottom of a page which is reused across several pages.

Headers usually contain a site's logo and will often have the site's navigation and a search box. Footers usually contain less important items like a copyright notice and links to the site's "terms and conditions" or "privacy policy".

The benefits of consistency

Your visitors will find your site easier to use if there's consistency from page to page. They'll also know they're still in your site and haven't been taken to another site by clicking on an external link.

Having a header and footer also saves you a lot of work as a web designer because you don't have to design and build the whole of each page, just the areas that are unique to the page.

Hot tip

You can create your header and footer once and then use *Server Side Includes* to add them to each of your pages.

When you need to update either the header or footer, you'll only have to change one file.

Navigation

Unless your website only has one page, your visitors will need a way of getting around. Each page should have a way for your visitors to navigate the site. Usually this will be a navigation bar at the top of the page (or on the left), with links to the main pages or sections.

Barnes & Noble's site, **bn.com**, is very large so it has two areas of navigation—along the top and to the left.

Don't forget

A site's navigation is just a collection of links grouped together in one area of the page.

I want my site navigation to be innovative

You might think it's dull to put your navigation bar at the top (like every other site), but your visitors expect to see it there.

Don't be different for the sake of it. Your visitors want to be able to find their way around your site, not to marvel at your "creativity". Ask yourself whether a novel way of navigating your site will help you achieve your goals or whether you've fallen into the trap of doing something just because you think it looks cool.

Search box

The first thing many people do when they come to a new site is to look for a search box. Why? Because it's quicker and easier to search for "contact details" than to look through the site for them.

If your site only has a few pages, you might feel you don't need a search, but if you've got more than a dozen pages, it's definitely worth considering allowing people to search your site.

Where should your search box go?

Most sites with search boxes put them in the top right-hand corner of the page, so this is the first place people look for them. Unless there's a good reason not to put it there, top right is probably the best place for your search box.

1 Most visitors expect to see a search box in the top right-hand corner of the web page.

Is adding a search box hard?

It doesn't need to be. Although larger sites will often get a web developer to write a specialized search program for their site, many sites rely on Google's free site search.

To find out how to set it up on your site, search Google for "Google co-op" or visit **www.google.com/coop/**

The disadvantage of using a free search tool like Google, is you can't completely control the way the result page looks and works.

If this is important to you, there are several search scripts you can download and customize. Some, like mnoGoSearch (**mnogosearch.org**) are free to use while others, like Site Search Pro (**site-search-pro.com**) are available for a small fee.

Pop-up windows

Pop-ups are extra windows that are opened by a web page in order to show another page. There are two types of pop-ups:

- Pop-ups that have been opened without the visitors permission (like pop-up adverts)

- Pop-ups that open after the visitor performs some action (like clicking on a link)

Because the pop-up windows that are opened automatically are usually associated with advertising, people find them very annoying and often close them before the page has even loaded. So it's generally a good idea to avoid these kind of pop-ups.

Having a window pop-up when your visitor clicks on a link, however, can be very useful–for instance, if they want to check your site's terms and conditions without leaving the page they're on. However, be sure to let them know they're opening a pop-up, otherwise they might get confused.

Hot tip

Instead of using pop-up windows you can create "in-page pop-ups" using css and Javascript.

These work in a similar way to pop-up windows but are part of the same page.

These are better as they're more accessible and still work when Javascript is turned off.

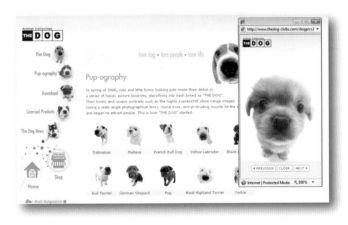

How pop-up windows work

Normally pop-up windows are opened by Javascript, although basic pop-ups can be opened using just HTML.

You can control the size and position of the window, the page it will open, whether it will include an address bar or toolbar and even whether the visitor is able to resize the pop-up.

Pop-ups can sometimes create problems for disabled visitors and can be confusing for web "newbies" as well, so use them with care.

Frames & scrolling areas

Most web pages are made up of one continuous area, a bit like a page in a book. However, it's sometimes useful to be able to have an area within a page which is independent of the rest of it, so that the visitor can scroll without moving the whole page.

Scrolling areas, like the one seen below on the ineasysteps.com homepage, can be useful if having a larger box would "break" the design of the page. They're also handy if you want your visitors to be able to see one area of the page at all times, like the navigation.

1 Ineasysteps.com uses a scrolling area to allow the page to show more than three best-selling books without breaking the design.

43

Frames vs. CSS

There are two ways to create scrolling areas on your page; using frames or css.

Traditionally, scrolling areas have been created using a technique called frames (or iframes) which places one web page *within* another. Although frames are very powerful, they have several disadvantages. For instance, they're awkward to create, don't do well in search engines and are difficult for disabled people to use.

A much better technique is to create scrolling areas using css. Although less commonly used, css scrolling areas are more elegant than frames and easier to implement.

The css code to create a scrolling area is actually very simple; you just need to edit the `overflow` property of the object you want to allow to scroll. Typically, it will be something like this:

Hot tip

For more information about frames, turn to page 158.

```
.scrollingarea {
  overflow: auto;
}
```

Advertising

Hate it or love it, advertising plays an integral part in the Web today, partly because it's the easiest way for websites which offer content (as opposed to selling things) to make money.

The most common type of online advertising is the *banner ad*. These are usually animated gifs or Flash animations which sit at the top or bottom of a web page. Technically, banner ads are advertisements that are wider than they are tall–but the term usually includes tall ads (*skyscraper ads*) as well.

Other common types of online advertising include *pop-ups* (very annoying, so best avoided), *interstitials* (ads that appear for a few seconds when you click on a link) and *AdWords* (see page 175).

Banner and skyscraper adverts are a common way for websites to make money. Since they sit within the web page, they need to fit within the overall design.

4 Writing for the Web

Without words, most websites couldn't exist. So, if you want your site to achieve your business goals, it's important you pay as much attention to the writing as the design.

Keep it short and simple

One of the main reasons people use the Web is to save time. It's quicker and easier to look up film times for your local multiplex on their website than to walk there and check the poster.

So, the last thing you want to do is force your visitors to wade through long wordy pages as this will slow them down. Chances are, they'll give up and go to another site if you do.

Keep your writing as short and to the point as possible. Think about things from your visitors' point of view. Why have they come to this page and what do they want to know? Let them have the information in the quickest way possible.

1 Ignoring the navigation, there are very few words on this page, making it quick and easy to read.

If you're not sure if there's a simpler way to say something, why not visit **thesaurus.com?**

Don't be too clever

Unless the goal of your site is to "impress people with the size of my vocabulary", don't use words that are unnecessarily long.

It doesn't matter whether your site's trying to sell novelty t-shirts, influence voters or encourage recycling: if people can't understand what you're trying to say, you will fail.

Even if you're writing for a specialist audience, like scientists or engineers, ask yourself if you're using longer words to help your site reach its goals or to make yourself sound clever.

Grab people with headlines

When you read a newspaper, you skim through it looking at headlines and photos to help you decide which stories you want to read in more depth and which to avoid. It's the same online.

People scan websites, using headlines (also called headings) to help them decide whether it's worth reading the whole page or not. If you want to give your copy a chance to be read, you need to make sure you use punchy, descriptive headlines.

Your headlines should sum up the contents of the page, while making people want to read more. Try to keep them as short and punchy as possible by cutting out any unnecessary words.

Plant keywords in your headlines

One way search engines rank your pages is by looking at the text in your page and especially headlines. If you want to be listed under "Denver iPod shop", it will help if you include those words in your headline, e.g. "Denver's favorite iPod shop".

Writing a news story

Newspaper journalists get straight to the point: they have to. People usually switch news stories after a few paragraphs, or sooner if it's boring. So, journalists have to get the main facts of the story across in the first few sentences.

The way people skim newspapers is a lot like the way they surf the Web, stopping to read stories that grab their attention and moving on as soon as they become bored. So, news stories are ideal for learning how to write attention-grabbing copy for web pages – and of course many websites have news stories on them.

The intro

The first sentence of a news story is more important than the rest of them put together. In 30 words, or less, you've got to grab the reader's attention and explain the basics of what happened. A boring intro can ruin a great story.

Start the drama from the first word

Try to make the first word of your news story as dramatic as possible. Which of these intros grabs you more?

Having already caused a record number of casualties this month, Shiite insurgents claimed 8 more victims…

Gunmen killed 8 people near a Baghdad mosque last night…

The five Ws (and an H)

After finishing your intro, the reader should understand the basics of what happened, so they shouldn't be left with any big questions.

To check you've covered everything, you should reread your intro and check you've answered these common questions:

- Who? Who died? Who shot him? Who won the Superbowl?
- What? What happened?
- When? When did this take place?
- Where? Where did it happen?
- Why? Why did they do it?
- How? How did they do it?

You'll almost always need to tell the reader what happened and who (or what) did it, but you won't always need to explain why or how it happened in the first sentence.

Hot tip

Try thinking of the intro to a news story as a trailer for a film. Imagine they made the news story into a movie. If you could show just one moment from the film, what would you show? That should be your intro.

Don't forget

You can use the techniques here in any piece of writing, not just an online news story.

Get straight to the point, use attention-grabbing words and answer all the reader's questions, then people will enjoy reading what you've written.

Use active sentences

To create a punchy news story, use lots of *active sentences*. These are sentences where a person (or thing) *does* something, usually to another person (or thing). For example:

The robber shot Mr. Smith.

is an active sentence, but:

Mr. Smith was shot by the robber.

isn't, it's a *passive sentence*.

Active sentences are more direct than passive sentences and make the story sound like it's just happened. If you find lots of words like *was* and *were* in your writing, you might be using too many passive sentences. See if you can rewrite any as active sentences.

Delete ~~any~~ unneeded words

To keep your ~~news~~ story as ~~short and to the point~~ concise as possible you should go through it to ~~take out~~ remove any words ~~that~~ you can, without significantly changing the meaning ~~of the sentence. To paraphrase George Orwell,~~ "Why use ten words when one will do?~~"~~

The rest of the story

OK, so you've written your intro. What next? Well the next paragraph, or two, should add information to the first. Then, if possible, you add a supporting quote. Something like this:

Toni Braxton will tour for the first time in 10 years, the R&B diva revealed recently.

The "Unbreak My Heart" singer will perform live around America later this year to promote her latest album, "Libra".

Braxton said, "I'm thrilled to be going out on the road again. I can't wait to bring not only the hits that people know and love but to share the new music from 'Libra' with the audience."

Then you repeat this structure for the second and third most important points about the story and add supporting information (Who is Toni Braxton? When's the last time she toured? Why did she stop?) Keep going until you've run out of things to say or until you've reached your word count – if you have one.

Sell anything in 4 steps

Most commercial sites are trying to sell something–either a product or a service. But how do you write great sales copy for your site?

One way is to adopt a technique used by professional salespeople, called AIDA. It stands for *Attention*, *Interest*, *Desire* and *Action*.

Attention

Before a salesperson can sell you anything, they need to get your *attention* and make a good first impression. First impressions count online too. People are more likely to trust a smart, professional-looking site than a poorly produced one.

Interest

Once a salesperson has your attention, they've got a short amount of time to grab your *interest*. Again, it's the same online.

The way salespeople try to get your interest is to identify a problem which their product will be able to solve. A salesperson might ask if you, "Find dusting the top of your dresser hard?" If you do, you can be sure their product will solve this problem.

One way to use this technique in your sales copy is to ask a rhetorical question and then illustrate or reinforce the problem with an example, a story or some facts and figures.

Do you worry about what will happen to your cats after you die? 90 per cent of cat owners do...

Desire

The next step for the salesperson is to get you to want (or *desire*) their product or service. They do this by telling you how it will solve the problem they've highlighted.

For example, they might tell you that, "The new SuperDuster has an extra long handle so you can dust those hard to reach places."

You can use this technique in your sales copy too.

Action

Convincing someone you've got a great product is one thing–getting to them to actually buy it is another.

Make sure you put a clear *call to action* on your sales pages, such as a "buy now" button or an instruction to "phone us today".

Don't forget

Your sales copy needs to take the reader through three steps:

1 Point out a problem

2 Show how your product will fix that problem

3 Ask your reader to buy your product

Painting with words

People often say that a picture paints a thousand words, but it doesn't usually take a thousand words to paint a picture of your product or service in somebody's mind.

Describe, don't oversell

It's often tempting to tell people how wonderful your product or service is, but why should they trust you? After all, you *are* biased. Don't be tempted to overuse so-called "power words" like *amazing*, *guaranteed* or *free*. You might think these will make your product sound great, but they're more likely to make you sound like a fraud. Don't make claims you can't back up either.

Instead, describe your product and let the reader make up their own mind. Compare these two product descriptions:

AMAZING new web design program! Double your hits—GUARANTEED! FREE key ring for every buyer!

Dreamweaver is the world's leading web design software. The latest version features dozens of new tools to make designing a website quicker and easier, including guidelines and a zoom tool. With built-in FTP and seamless integration with other Macromedia products, like Flash, Dreamweaver is a must-have web design tool.

Highlight the benefits, not the features

People often make the mistake of listing the features, not the benefits, of their product or service.

Consumers buy things because of the *benefits* they provide. A coat keeps them warm, a car takes them long distances quickly and an iPod lets them listen to music anywhere. Of course, the benefit doesn't have to be practical. Perhaps they bought a new coat and iPod to make themselves look cool or feel better?

Ask yourself why people buy things from *you*. For example, if you sell coats, do people buy them because your coats are very warm or because they look stylish?

Then, describe the benefits of your product, not their features. Which of these two sentences describes the benefits better?

Our coats will keep you warm even on the frostiest winter day.

Using patented ThermoFortress technology, the TF3000i high-density ski-coat is the ultimate all-terrain jacket.

Beware

It's very easy to appear pushy or insincere when you CAPITALIZE words or overuse exclamation marks!

Why search engines matter

Unless you're a household name, like CNN or eBay, most people will find your site through a search engine, so it's important to get a good search engine *ranking*.

How well your site performs in search engines depends on several factors, including the way the site's HTML is coded and the number of other websites linking to it. However, one of the key things they look at is the text used on the site.

Hot tip

For more in-depth info on how search engines work, go to Chapter 16.

How does your writing affect search ranking?

When you type a word or phrase into a search engine it tries to show you a list of relevant web pages. The important word is *relevant*. If you search for "New York dentist" then ideally you'd like a page full of websites for dentists in New York.

One way to tell if a web page is relevant is to look at the writing it contains. If a page contains the phrase "New York dentist", then it's more likely to be relevant than one that doesn't. This is how the earliest search engines worked and is still important today.

Should I change the way I write?

Not drastically, no, but you do need to be aware of how search engines are going to examine your writing. Choose two or three words, or phrases, which people might type into Google when looking for a site like yours.

Hot tip

For more advice and information on writing for search engines, visit **searchenginewatch.com**

Then, work these *keywords* into the first few hundred words of your page several times. Try to work them into your page title and headings, as well as the body copy. Don't overload your page with your keywords or Google will assume you're trying to cheat.

Do you trust your spelling?

For your website to achieve your goals people need to trust you. Whether you want them to buy a DVD or listen to your views on global warming, if people don't trust you it'll be hard to succeed.

The quickest way to lose people's trust is to have mistakes on your site, so it's vital you thoroughly check your spelling and grammar. After all, if somebody can't be bothered to check their spelling, would you really trust them to look after your credit card details?

Use a spell checker

It's amazing how often websites have typos. Every modern word processor and web design program has a spell checker, so there's no excuse.

Learn the difference between *its* and *it's*

It's is short for *it is* or *it has*. *Its* means "belonging to it". Don't get the two confused.

It's hard to find talented writers these days.

The puppy loved its owner.

Should you have less mistakes or fewer?

It's easy to get words with similar meanings confused. For example, do you know the difference between *less* and *fewer*? You generally use *fewer* with things you can count (cars, CDs, apples) and *less* with things you can measure (oil, flour, water).

I have less water than George and fewer apples.

Get a second opinion

It's always easier to spot someone else's mistakes than your own. Get another person to check over your site, ideally someone who's good at spelling and grammar.

Use a style guide

There are often several correct ways to say something. 10 per cent, 10 percent and 10% are all correct, but it would look strange if you used all three in the same sentence.

To make your site look professional you should decide on a set of rules to use and then stick to them. Larger sites often create a *style guide* for writers, with rules on everything from spelling and punctuation, to what to call the Queen of England.

Beware

Spelling mistakes could damage your site's search engine ranking, as well as its credibility.

You'll also make it hard for blind people to use your site, as their *screen reader* software won't know how to pronounce misspelt words.

Hot tip

Here are some words people often confuse as they sound alike:

- There, their & they're
- To, too & two
- Your & you're
- Accept & except
- Affect & effect

Hot tip

There are several good online style guides you could use. Search Google for the *Chicago Manual of Style* or the *BBC News Styleguide*.

Top 9 web writing tips

1 Get to the point

People don't want to waste time online reading waffle. Say what you need to, clearly and quickly–then stop.

2 Use a spell checker...

There's no excuse for typos. Your web design software should have a spell checker and if it doesn't, you can copy and paste your site's content into Word.

3 ...but don't rely on it

Your spell checker will pick up typos like "tommorrow" but it won't spot real words you've used incorrectly.

4 Avoid jargon

The point of having a website is to reach as many people as possible–not to confuse them. If you can't avoid jargon and acronyms, provide an explanation of their meaning.

5 Use headings to help people skim read

Headings help people decide whether to read a page or to find specific content within it. Well written headings can really improve the user-friendliness of a site.

6 Keep your paragraphs short

Short paragraphs encourage people to read more, especially towards the end of a page, when their attention is drifting.

7 Remember search engines

Write for your visitors but don't forget that search engines will look at your copy too. Dropping keywords into headings and body copy will help your ranking.

8 Ensure links make sense

To help search engines and blind visitors, ensure your links make sense. "Click here" is meaningless on its own, so say "click here for our contact form" instead.

9 Get a friend to check for mistakes

It's much easier to spot someone else's mistakes than your own, so get a friend or colleague to check your site for you.

5 The rules of good design

There's a lot involved with creating a website. You might need to know Photoshop, Dreamweaver, HTML or even PHP and MySQL. But how do you design a good site? In this chapter you'll learn the rules of web design and how you can apply them to create an attractive and effective website.

Pencil & Paper (the ultimate web design tools)

Computers are fantastic tools for designers, but there's nothing like the speed and simplicity of a piece of paper and a pencil when it comes to coming up with creative ideas.

The most important part of any design is the ideas that lie behind it. Before you even touch a computer, you should sit down with a pad and sketch your ideas.

Sketching helps you clarify and refine your thoughts and allows you to show them to other people (like your boss) for feedback.

As well as sketches, list any ideas you've got. You can include everything from a simple sitemap to the names of other sites you admire.

Ideally, you'll be able to do this with at least one other person, so you can bounce ideas off each other. The best ideas often come from this kind of creative brainstorming.

One great thing with sketches is they're quick to create and quick to alter, so if you decide to take a different direction you haven't wasted hours, or even days, at the computer.

Don't worry about the quality of your drawing, as the important thing is to get the ideas down on paper. You'll probably want to do several different initial designs and then several versions of your chosen design.

This early sketch for **ineasysteps.com** (right) shows how the layout evolved during the design process.

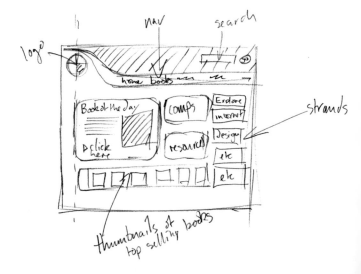

How big is a web page?

Paper always stays the same size. Every page of this book, for example, is 186mm wide and 227mm high.

A web page, on the other hand, changes size depending on the computer you use to look at it. Different computers have different sized screens.

Screen sizes are measured in pixels and the smallest ones are 640 pixels wide and 480 pixels high (640 x 480). Screens this small are quite rare these days – most people's computers are 800 x 600 or 1024 x 768.

This website is too wide for 1 in 5 people's screens

One of the first decisions you need to make when you're designing your site is how big to make the pages.

If your page is larger than the visitor's screens, he or she will have to scroll to see the rest of it. Most people don't mind scrolling down but you normally shouldn't make them scroll sideways.

Because of this, it's important to decide on the width of your web pages. If it's too wide, your visitor will have to scroll horizontally.

Most web designers choose to design for 800 x 600 screens, so they'll make the page 770 pixels wide or less (to leave space for the scrollbar). However, if your site is aimed at people that are likely to have larger screens, like graphic designers, it may be safe to design for a 1024 x 768 screen.

Don't forget

Websites don't have to be a fixed width. Some web designers prefer "liquid layouts", which expand to fit your browser window.

Others use "elastic layouts", which expand based on the size of the text, allowing people to zoom in.

Getting to grips with the grid

If you look at any two pages of this book you'll notice certain similarities. For instance, the page numbers are in the same place, the headings are the same size and the left-hand edge of the text is aligned with the left-hand edge of the page title.

That's because this book, like almost every other book on the market, uses a *grid* to guide the way elements are positioned on the page.

Grids are basically a plan for your page, whether it's a web page or the page of a book. You can't normally see them, but here we've left the grid showing. It's marked by the light blue dotted lines.

Look closely at any magazine, newspaper, website or poster and you'll see that most designers use a grid to guide the layout of their designs.

Kananipearl.com uses two layouts based on the same 5-column grid.

The gray *wireframes* below show the basic structure of each layout.

What's the point of having a grid?

Grids perform three important functions in websites. First, they give your design structure and balance.

Second, they create consistency from page to page, which means it's easier for visitors to use your site. Knowing where the navigation, content and sidebars are going to appear, from one page to the next, helps them navigate your site quickly and means your site's more likely to achieve your business goals.

Third, because of the way HTML works, sites that are designed to a grid will be much easier to code.

So how do I use grids?

Planning a grid is one of the first things you should do when you're designing a website.

Most web designers use a graphics package like Photoshop or Fireworks to design their pages. These programs let you create guidelines which you can use to align objects to your grid. Any major elements on your page, like headings, text and images, should line up with one or more of these guidelines.

Don't grids create "blocky" designs?

They can – but only if used unimaginatively. Soul singer Joss Stone's site uses quite a simple grid, which gives it structure, but the extensive use of curves means it doesn't seem at all "square".

Hot tip

Copying other people's designs is obviously wrong, but there's no harm in using a similar grid to someone else.

Look at other sites you like and see if you can work out the grid they're using. Would something similar suit your site?

59

The key to using grids is to let them guide you, but not to be constrained by them.

The Art of Typography

We use words because they mean something to us. However, it's not just the dictionary definition of a word that affects our understanding of it. The shape of the letters and the relationship between them also influences the way we interpret words.

What is a font?

When most people use the word "font" they actually mean "typeface". A *typeface* is a design for the alphabet, numbers and punctuation marks. Typefaces come in different sizes (11pt, 8pt) and varieties (**bold**, *italic*). A *font* is the name for a specific use of a typeface. Arial is a typeface and **Arial Bold 9pt** is a font.

Just add structure

Good typography should look attractive, but it should also help the reader to *use* the words on your page. Typography can add structure to your web page, helping the reader navigate it.

For example, when you first opened this page, you probably looked at the page title first, as it was much bigger and heavier than the other type on the page. Then, perhaps, you glanced over the sub-headings, which are larger than the surrounding text, as well as being in a different color and typeface.

By guiding your eyes towards key phrases like this, the designer introduces the subject of the page before you've read it.

The bold and the beautiful

One of the most obvious ways you can draw attention to certain words is to make them **bold**. As they're heavier and darker than ordinary type, the reader's eye will be drawn towards bold words.

Italics also draw attention to words, but they can subtly change the way they're interpreted, so you should use them sparingly. You should also use italics for certain names and titles.

A change of typeface can drastically alter our interpretation of a sentence.

The words "God save the Queen" would normally make you think the writer was a monarchist, but by using "punkier" typefaces your reader will be left with the opposite impression.

Types of typeface

There are thousands of typefaces available so it helps to put them into categories:

Serif

Times New Roman

Sans-serif

Arial

Serif typefaces like Times New Roman have small flourishes called serifs on them, while sans-serif ones like Arial don't.

Graphic

Mistral

Monospaced

Courier

Typefaces like this are only good for short bursts of text.

Each letter fits into the same character width.

Becoming a control freak

As well as choosing which typefaces to use on your site, you need to decide how to use them. As a designer, you can control the size of the letters you use, their position on the page and the distance between them.

How you control these relationships will affect how well your site's message comes across and, ultimately, how successful it is.

The space race

The relationship between words and letters is less obvious than the size and typeface used, but it's just as important. Altering the space between letters, lines and words can improve their impact and legibility.

Changing the space between individual letters is called *kerning*. Use it in headings to reduce ugly gaps between letters (Yo to Yo).

C h a n g i n g   t h e   s p a c e   b e t w e e n   e v e r y   l e t t e r   i s   c a l l e d   *t r a c k i n g*.

Changing the space between lines is called *leading* (pronounced led-ing). Extra space can make the text easier to read. In fact, *legibility* is one of the most important functions of typography. After all, words aren't much use if we can't read them.

Hot tip

Each typeface has its own "personality".

Choose one that suits the message you want to convey to your readers.

Professional

Garamond

Clean

Avenir

Powerful

Impact

Friendly

RickysHand

Futuristic

Eurostyle

Elegant

Edwardian Script ITC

Retro

Bauhaus 93

Typed

TypewriterRough

Fun

Curlz MT

Fonts on the Web

The Web was originally created by scientists to share physics papers. Worthwhile as this was, unfortunately, it meant HTML wasn't created with typographers in mind.

Graphic designers and typographers are used to having lots of control over type, but HTML doesn't give you nearly as many options as you'd have with even a simple word processor. You can't fit text to a curve, position type precisely or add drop shadows. In fact, you can't even choose the exact font to use.

This might be frustrating, but for the time being it's something web designers have to live with.

So what *can* you do?

Well, using CSS you can control the size, color and position of text on the page and the spacing between letters and lines.

You can also specify the typeface to use. However, because you don't actually send the font with the HTML page, the visitor needs to have the font installed on their computer, if it's to appear as you originally intended. In practice, this means you've only got a few fonts to choose from: Times New Roman / Times, Arial / Helvetica, Verdana, Trebuchet, Georgia and Courier.

Can you read it?

While it's important for text to look attractive, it's vital that people can read it easily. There are several things you can do to improve the legibility of the text on your page:

- **Size**
  Make sure the text is large enough for your *target audience* to read. If your site is aimed at old people the text will need to be larger than if it's aimed at teenagers.

- **Contrast**
  Red text on a black background is hard to see, so if you want people to read what you've written then don't use it. Dark text on a light background is easiest for most people to read.

- **Leading**
  Increasing the space between lines (or *leading*) slightly can improve the legibility of your text. It's very easy to set the leading using CSS.

```
body { line-height: 1.5; }
```

Hot tip

If you want more control over your text than HTML allows, you can use CSS to replace text with *images* of text made in a program like Photoshop.

Only use this technique on headings though, as images can't be resized, like text can.

Websites aren't printed on paper

Web design has a lot in common with graphic design. You probably want your website to look attractive, enforce your brand and tempt people into purchasing your products.

However, there are some significant differences between print and the Web as a medium, which you need to understand before you start designing websites.

The most obvious difference between websites and print is that websites appear on a computer screen. Computer screens are much *lower resolution* than printed documents, meaning they look less sharp. A typical brochure or business card will be printed at a resolution of 300dpi (dots per inch), whereas most computer screens are only 72dpi.

Learn to let go

One of the biggest differences between designing websites and designing brochures, posters or magazine spreads is that you have much less control over the way your pages will appear.

People will look at your sites using different types of computer, at different screen sizes, using different browsers and with different types of monitor. Some people set up their computers to make the text larger or ignore the colors and fonts you chose, as they have poor eyesight. Other people will look at your site on their PDA or cell phone. Some won't look at it at all, they'll listen to it using a *screen reader*, designed for blind people. Sometimes it won't even be a person looking at your website, but a computer program, like Google.

Every single person that looks at your website will get a slightly different experience and you don't get to decide exactly what they see. At first, this seems like a limitation of web design, but it's actually its strength.

Imagine a printed brochure that could be translated automatically into dozens of major languages, read by the blind and even automatically scanned into a computer and then delivered anywhere in the world (at virtually no cost to you) to people who had already expressed an interest in your product or service.

Wouldn't that be neat? Well that's what websites do—and it's precisely because you don't have 100% control over the way they're shown that they're able to do all this and more.

Don't forget

Websites also handle colors in a different way from printed designs. They're designed in RGB, rather than CMYK.

RGB stands for red, green and blue, while CMYK stands for cyan, magenta, yellow and black (key). If you don't already know the difference, don't worry; it's just a different way of handling colors.

63

U s i n g

How do you decide which colors to use on your website? One way is just to choose ones you like. If you're lucky, the colors you select could end up looking nice together. Unless you've got a natural talent for choosing them, though, it's easy to create a color scheme that clashes.

Understanding color

To some extent, color is subjective. After all, everyone has a different favorite, don't they? However, there are many things to consider when choosing colors and various techniques that you can use to help choose a color palette for your site.

Grabbing people's attention

Color can help you make money. People's eyes get drawn towards strong colors like orange, red and lime green, especially when there are only one or two patches of them on a page.

You can use strong colors in combination with other graphic design devices (like unusual shapes or positioning), to draw attention to certain elements on a web page. If you draw people's attention to your *call to action*, like a phone number or "buy now" button (see page 76), your website is likely to be more successful.

Color and culture

Red means danger, gold is the color of wealth and green signifies environmentalism. Why? Well, there are often good reasons (fire is red, plants are green) but essentially, the reason colors carry meaning is that everybody within a culture thinks they do.

Don't forget, other cultures attach different meanings to colors, so it's important to be aware of them if you're designing for an international audience. For example, in Ireland, orange is associated with protestantism and in the Far East, white, rather than black, is associated with mourning.

The psychology of color

Color also has a subconscious influence on our mood. Reds and oranges are warm, while blues are cold. Advertisers, interior designers and film makers have been using color for years to subtly influence our mood. For example, the film *The Matrix* has a strong green tint (the color of a circuit board) whenever a scene is set in virtual reality, giving it a clinical, technological feel.

64

Color wheels help you choose colors that work well together.

c o l o r

However, the scenes set in the real world have a blue tint, emphasizing the cold reality of the situation.

Color strengthens your brand

Colors help people instantly recognize your company. Firms like Starbucks, Ferrari and McDonalds are identified with their corporate colors as well as their logos. Coca-Cola cans are so well-known for their distinctive shade of red that most other brands of cola have followed suit and use red cans too.

When it comes to color, less is more

One of the mistakes people often make when they first start designing is using too many colors. Pick one main color and then use one or two others to complement it. Using *tints* of the same color (lighter or darker shades) is another reliable approach.

Color theory

Artists, designers and photographers use various rules, known collectively as *color theory*, to help them choose combinations of colors that work well together.

One of the most useful tools in color theory is the *color wheel*, like the one on the opposite page. Color wheels help you choose colors that work well together.

For example, colors which lie opposite each other on the color wheel (called *complementary colors*) work well together, as do colors that are close to each other on the wheel (*analogous colors*).

Choosing a color palette

Before you start designing your site, it's helpful to create a color palette to use.

If you're designing a site for a company that is already in business, the palette will probably be based on their existing corporate color scheme.

If you're designing a site for yourself, you should choose colors that create a mood that will suit your website. Think about your business goals for the site and the look-and-feel you're trying to convey to your visitors.

Don't forget

Websites use RGB color, rather than CMYK (see page 63).

Shakira.com uses a small number of colors that work well together.

The crimson, orange and yellow give the site a warm, friendly and feminine feel.

All three colors are close on the color wheel. In other words, they're analogous colors.

Lines & shapes

Lines and shapes are useful for helping to organize your web pages visually into different sections. They help make the page more interesting and easier for the visitor to use.

Lines

Lines are one of the most fundamental elements you can use to design a web page. In web design, they're most often used to organize the page. However, they can also be used to guide people's eyes towards certain parts of it, as people naturally follow a line from one end to the other.

1. On this page from **corkd.com**, lines are used to divide up the page, as well as to ornament sub-headings.

2. Shapes, like this white rectangle, are also commonly used to organize pages into sections.

3. Shapes can be created in a variety of ways. This illustration of a wine bottle creates a shape on the page, which grabs your attention.

There are various types of line. Some of the options include: straight, curved, thick, thin, dotted, dashed, solid and textured. Choose carefully, as the lines you use will affect the overall mood of your design. For example, thin lines can look elegant while a textured line might appear casual.

Shapes

Like lines, shapes are often used in web design to help organize the page. Splitting a design into sections makes it easier to use as your visitors have less information to take in at once.

Shapes allow you to guide people's eyes towards parts of the page which are important. For example, you may want to draw attention to your "buy now" button or phone number.

If your design is mostly made up of rectangles, then making one element a circle, star or triangle will draw attention to it.

Gradients & texture

Gradients have become very fashionable in web design over recent years. They help make large areas of color less imposing and can help draw the visitor's eyes in the right direction.

They're also useful for organizing the page into different sections, without creating a "boxy" look-and-feel.

1 Rather than using a solid box, the designer of **blogger.com** employed gradients to "suggest" sections on the page. Notice how your eyes follow the direction of the gradient downwards.

It's usually best to avoid going from one color to a totally different one, as they might clash. Gradients between different shades of the same color (e.g. light blue to darker blue) or from a light color to white can work very well, though.

Texture

Texture is very important in print design, but it's under-used on the Web. This is partly because websites don't get printed, so don't have any built-in texture like paper does.

However, texture can still be used to great effect on websites. Background images of paper or fabric can give a website an old-fashioned feel. Be careful if you use this technique, though, as there's a fine line between an attractive website and a very tacky one.

As with everything in your design, you should only use texture if it helps you achieve the overall goal of your site and enhances your desired look-and-feel.

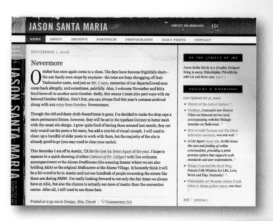

Thanks to Jason Santa Maria
www.jasonsantamaria.com

Size & contrast

One key aspect of web design is to draw people's attention towards elements on the page you want them to look at, like a "buy now" button or phone number.

Two highly effective ways to do this are to make the most important elements bigger than other elements on the page, or to make them contrast with surrounding elements.

1 The "Book of the day" on the **waterstones.com** homepage takes up a larger area than any other element on the page, giving it more prominence.

2 Other products take up less space on the page, so appear less important.

People are naturally drawn towards the largest area on a web page and subconsciously assume that it is more important that other areas of the page.

Contrast

Similarly, people's eyes naturally get drawn to any element that contrasts with other elements on the page.

The darkness (or lightness) of any element is known, by graphic designers, as its *value*. If your page is mostly light, then dark elements will draw the visitor's attention.

Value isn't the only way to create contrast. You can use unusual colors or shapes to attract people towards certain elements. A bright orange star on a page that is mostly navy blue and rectangular will stand out. Make sure you use contrast sparingly, though, or your visitors won't know where to look.

Screenshot from **ktsplc.com**

Position is everything

Unlike printed documents, web pages can be scrolled. When you first look at a long page, you will only be able to see the top few inches of it, so if there are any elements you definitely want people to see, it's important to place them *above the fold*.

The expression "above the fold" comes from the world of journalism. Newspapers are commonly folded in half to get them on news stands, so the main story on the front page needs to be "above the fold", in order to be seen by shoppers.

On a web page, an element is "above the fold" if it can be seen without scrolling. Exactly where "the fold" is depends on the size of your visitor's screen, but it's usually between 450 and 650 pixels down the page.

1 The "fold" is the lowest part of a web page that can be seen without scrolling. Important elements should be placed "above the fold", with less important ones "below the fold".

2 Hotspots are areas of a web page people are more likely to look at.

Placing important elements of your design, such as product promotions, in a hotspot means more people will notice them.

Certain positions on a web page are much more likely to be looked at than others. The main *hotspot* on a page is a few inches down and to the right of the top left-hand corner. Any element placed there will get noticed quicker and by more people, so make sure you place your most important one there.

Guiding people's eyes

People who speak English read from left to right and from top to bottom. This means the first place they look on a web page is the top left-hand corner.

One of the most important jobs of a web designer is to steer people towards certain parts of the page (like the "buy now" button) using visual clues.

How do people look at a web page?
People's eyes flick around the page when it first loads, settling on some parts for a few seconds and then moving on.

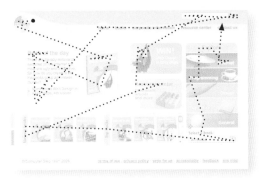

The dotted purple line shows the path a typical visitor's eyes might follow when looking at the **ineasysteps.com** homepage.

The visitor's eyes start in the top left-hand corner of the page and then zig-zag their way down and to the right.

What does this mean for web designers?
The top-left of the page is the first place people look and it's the area they look at hardest, so it's an ideal place to put important content that you don't want people to miss.

People's eyes are drawn to certain elements
When you walk down the street, your attention is naturally drawn towards certain things: a striking billboard ad, a coin somebody's dropped or an attractive member of the opposite sex.

When you visit a web page it's a similar experience. Your eyes are naturally drawn towards certain regions of the page and ignore others. Headings, patches of color and pictures of people's faces all tend to grab the eye.

As a web designer, it's important to understand this, so you can guide your visitors to parts of the page you want them to notice.

Don't forget

In the west, people read from top to bottom and left to right.

You've been trained to look at the top left-hand corner of every page you read since you were a small child, so it's no surprise that people look at that part of a web page first.

Where people look (and where they don't)

There are certain *hotspots* on a web page, where your visitors are much more likely to look than others.

People look at regions of the page where they expect to see content and ignore areas where they expect decoration or ads.

They usually look at the top left-hand corner first and then focus heavily on large headings, long passages of text and images of people's faces. For more information about which areas of a web page people look at, visit: **www.poynterextra.org/eyetrack2004/**

1. Research has shown that people don't tend to look at banner ads.

   Make sure nothing on your page looks like advertising if it isn't, or they may ignore that too.

2. Large headlines tend to draw people's attention.

3. People's eyes get drawn towards photographs of human faces, especially if they're large ones.

4. Shorter paragraphs (3-5 lines) encourage people to read further, especially as they get further down the page and their attention drops off.

Meeting people's expectations

Most websites have navigation along the top or down the left-hand side, so people will expect your navigation to be there.

If you put navigation on the right-hand side or at the bottom of the page, most people (but not all), will probably find it, but they'll waste time looking for it when they could be reading your content or clicking the "buy now" button. Likewise, the search box is usually top right and the logo is top left.

Attention to detail

The difference between an average website and a well-designed one often comes down to attention to detail. Little touches can make a big difference when it comes to the success of your site.

If you make sure elements line up, use fonts and colors that match and use consistent vocabulary on all your pages, then this gives your site an extra feeling of quality.

1 Many of the elements on the **authenticjobs. com** homepage line up, which isn't an accident.

2 Notice how the colors of the words "Established 2005" are mirrored in the words "Cameron Moll", on the other side of the page.

3 The typeface used in the logo is also used in the "Full Time" and "Freelance" column headings.

4 The exact shade of orange used in the strapline, under the logo, is used throughout the page. Likewise, the same shade of red is used in the header and the heading of the first column.

5 The curves used at the bottom of the sidebar are similar in style to those used in the logo.

Of course, it's not just the graphic design of a site that benefits from attention to detail. The best web designers think through every last aspect of a site from the visitor's point of view.

Many companies hire a copywriter to write product descriptions for their site, but what about hiring one to write the error messages? "Sorry, you've tried to look at a page that doesn't exist," is so much friendlier than "404 Error: See system administrator for details," don't you think?

Many people try to make their site look wonderful on a Windows PC, but why not go that extra mile and make sure the page still looks attractive on a PDA (see page 157) or when printed?

Less is more

When you start doing web design, it's tempting to try to put every idea you've ever had into your very first design. You might want drop shadows on all your images, funky "gel" buttons (like they have on the Apple website), a drop down menu, a Flash intro and a streaming video of the kitchen sink.

If that describes you, then great! It's fantastic that you're fired up about web design. However, try to resist the temptation of packing everything into your designs.

The best web designers give their designs room to "breathe", using plenty of *whitespace*. Whitespace doesn't have to be white, it's just the name for the areas of the design that are empty.

Web design blog **designbyfire.com** uses whitespace to great effect

If a design is too crowded, your eyes don't know where to look. Carefully-used whitespace helps guide your visitor's eyes towards the elements that you, as the designer, want them to see.

Sometimes, it helps to take a step back from your designs and ask yourself which elements are vital to have on the page and which aren't really necessary, in order to achieve the business goals you set for the site.

If you can't think of a compelling reason for something to be on your page, perhaps it shouldn't be there?

Web design is product design

Many people think of web design as being closely related to graphic design, or even just another branch of the profession.

Look in your local Yellow Pages and you'll find dozens of graphic designers offering websites as one of their long list of services, along with logo design, business cards and brochures.

This is fundamentally the wrong approach to designing websites. Web design is not a branch of graphic design, it's much closer to product design.

Websites have to *work*

Brochures, magazine ads, signs, logos and posters all differ from websites in one crucial respect; people don't have to *use* them.

All designers have to make sure their work is attractive, but product designers need to ensure their products are also easy to use and have features that people want.

A cell phone, for example, needs to be attractive, or consumers wouldn't buy it. However, people also need to be able to use it. There would be little point in having an attractive phone if you weren't able to call people because the speaker wasn't loud enough for you to hear, or the buttons were too small for you to press.

People also choose cell phones based on the features they offer. Most phones these days come with a color screen, built-in camera and several games.

Like cell phones, websites need to be easy to use and offer people features they want. Being attractive is important too, but in most cases it's not the *most* important thing.

Of course, graphic design isn't just about making things pretty—there's a lot more to it than that.

The difference between graphic design and product design (or web design) is that the objects designed by graphic designers don't have to be used (at least in any complicated way); they are simply looked at and read.

Beware

Graphic designers already have lots of the skills and knowledge to become good web designers.

However, don't make the mistake of thinking websites are just online brochures. They're not.

Just as there's more to print design than creating pretty layouts in Quark, there's more to web design than creating attractive designs in Photoshop and Dreamweaver.

Features, function and form

Websites, like products, can be looked at from three angles: features, function and form.

1 **Features**

The features of a product are often the most important aspect. When the cordless kettle was invented, people bought it because it did something other kettles couldn't.

A good website needs to *do something* that people want. The BBC website gives people up-to-the-minute news, while Google helps them find web pages they would be interested in. Even a 3-page, small business website lets people do something, i.e. find out about the company.

2 **Function**

The next aspect of any product (or website) is how well it works and how easy it is to use. Dyson vacuum cleaners do the same as any of their competitors; they suck up dust. However, they've sold well because they suck up dust much more efficiently than most other vacuum cleaners.

Likewise, Google wasn't the first search engine, but it has been phenomenally successful because it was easier to use and produced better search results than its competitors.

3 **Form**

The final aspect of any product is how it looks. Whether the aesthetics of a product are important depends on how similar its features and function are to its competitors.

iPods do a very similar job to every other MP3 player, but they've been successful because they look stunning, despite costing more. By contrast, the first Xerox wasn't particularly attractive, but it sold in huge numbers because, in 1959, it was the only automatic copier on the market.

People often use ugly websites that offer something their competitors don't. eBay isn't the best-looking site, but because so many people use it, it's a very effective way of buying and selling things. Of course, you should try to create attractive sites, but looks aren't everything.

Don't forget

While products are being developed, the designers make prototypes so they can test how well the product works and how easy to use it is.

You should also create prototypes of your websites and get real people to test them (see page 129 for more).

The call to action

When somebody visits your website, you should have an *action* in mind, which you want them to take. For example, you might want them to buy an Afghan carpet or call your sales team.

For your site to be successful, it's important to design every page with this action in mind.

You can't assume your visitors will realize, by themselves, what you want them to do. So, you need to ask them. You should put an explicit *call to action* on your pages, like a "buy now" button or a message saying, "Call us at 1-800-orangutan."

1 The call to action on this page from jewelry shop **fionaluing.co.uk** is well positioned, as it comes straight under the content.

Making it a brighter color or an unusual shape would have made the "add to cart" button even more visible.

76

It's important that people notice the call to action. So, don't be timid when you design it. Web design isn't about subtlety, it's about achieving the business goals you set for the website. People are much more likely to notice a bright orange star burst underneath the content than a stylish beige icon in the sidebar.

The best place to put the call to action is underneath the page content, but you can place additional calls to action in other places on the page.

Once you've designed your pages, print them out and test them on a few potential customers. First, ask them to look at the design for 5-10 seconds. Then, take it away and ask them to tell you what actions they could perform from the page. If they didn't notice your call to action, you need to redesign it.

Ugly websites make money

If you were to ask designers (or anyone else for that matter) to list the most attractive sites on the Web, few would mention Google, eBay, MySpace, Yahoo or Amazon. Yet these companies are worth billions. Why?

The answer's really simple – substance is much, much more important than style on the Web.

Many of the companies that collapsed during the **.com** bubble had beautiful websites. However, if you don't have a good concept, a workable business model, an easy-to-use website, interesting content, marketable products, reliable delivery, a genuine potential market and effective marketing, then it doesn't matter how pretty your site looks, it will unquestionably fail.

Beware

Websites that focus too hard on looking good, at the expense of being useful and easy to use, usually fail.

77

So, should I design an ugly website?

Of course not! The fact that ugly sites make money doesn't mean your website *must* look ugly in order to be successful, far from it. It simply means that looks are a minor factor in determining the success of most websites.

If you focus on aesthetics at the expense of more important factors, like usability, content and customer service, then your site is unlikely to meet the goals you set.

However, if you create an easy to use site with interesting content and effective marketing, *as well as* good design, then you're well on your way to creating a successful website.

The trick is to try to design a site that would succeed even if it was ugly – and then make it look attractive. The look-and-feel should be the icing on the cake.

Convention & style

Nobody wants their website to look ugly or boring. So, it's tempting to look at sites you don't find attractive and think, "I'm going to do the complete opposite."

However, the key to successful web design (in most cases) is to use a conventional layout and structure, but employ your graphic design skills to make the page look more attractive.

The *In Easy Steps* website actually uses a very conventional layout. For example, the navigation runs along the top, the search is top-right, there's a breadcrumb trail (see page 101), two columns and the content uses a heading and sub-headings.

The layout on the left looks ugly compared to **ineasysteps.com**, however both use the same basic structure for the page.

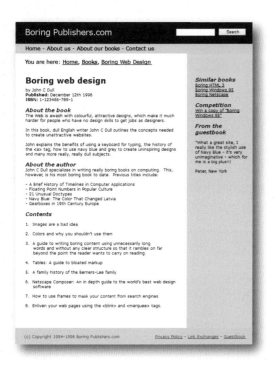

However, by carefully using colors, imagery and good typography, a run-of-the-mill layout has been transformed into an attractive and distinctive website.

Always ask, 'why'?

If you're planning to do something unconventional, ask yourself why. If putting the navigation on the right-hand side will help you achieve your site's business goals, that's fine, but if you're just being unconventional for the sake of it, it's probably a mistake.

6 Adding pictures

Without images, most websites would look very dull. In this chapter, you'll learn how to use photos, icons and illustrations to enhance your site.

How to take a good photo

It's impossible to teach you how to take a good photo in just one page, but here are some tips to help you improve your pictures:

Composition

Before you take a photo, it's important to think about the *composition* (where objects are placed in the photo).

One way to take an interesting shot is to make sure the main subject of photo is off-center.

In this shot, the girl's face is a third of the way up the photo and a third of the way in.

When you look though your viewfinder, try to imagine four lines a third of the way into the photo, like those on the picture.

If you place the subject of your picture on one of the four points, where these lines intersect, your photo will be more interesting.

Make sure you've got enough light

There's nothing worse than a photo that's too dark. If you're photographing some products for your site and the room isn't light enough, then take them outside.

Choose interesting colors

Colors evoke emotions in people. Look for strong patches of color and make them central to your photograph. Try not to overload your photos with too many colors; go for two or three that work well together.

A pile of fruit could have been a boring subject, but the colors and pattern make this an interesting photo.

Look for patterns

People love spotting patterns. Look for any patterns in the subject of your photograph and try to capture them.

Don't forget the basics

There's no way to guarantee you'll take a good photo, but there are plenty of ways to guarantee you won't. Make sure your subject is in focus and the photo is correctly *exposed*, so it's not too dark.

Choosing images for your site

Whenever you add anything to your website, you should first ask yourself *why* you're doing it. So, before you can choose which images to place on your site, you need to decide what the point of having them there is. Ask yourself:

- Do your images need to convey any information?
- Are they just for decoration?
- Do you want them to support the message of the words?
- What impression are you trying to create?
- Will they need to be updated, using a content management system?

Once you have a clear idea of the purpose of having images on your site, you can start to narrow down the kind of pictures that would be appropriate.

For example, if the images are going to be updated by somebody else, using a content management system, you may need to choose rectangular ones, so they're not forced to use Photoshop.

Keep it simple

Complex, detailed images might look wonderful on a brochure or a billboard, but they almost never work well online, as images on websites are much smaller and their quality is lower than in print.

Close-ups work well, as do simple images with a clear focus. Try not to get too hung up on imagery, though. Unless you are a photographer, people probably haven't come to your site to look at the pictures.

Buy one image

One great trick, if you're on a budget, is to buy one large, detailed image and show close-ups of different parts of it on individual pages of your site, rather than buying a separate image for each page.

As well as saving money, this trick helps you to maintain a consistent look-and-feel to your website.

Scanning & digital photos

If you plan to take photos for your website yourself, you'll either need to take them with a traditional camera and then scan them, or use a digital camera – but which method is better?

Scanning photos

Scanning photos is obviously slower and more expensive than using a digital camera, as you have to buy film, develop it and pay for prints. However, with a high-quality camera, the results from traditional photography can be very impressive.

Depending on the type of scanner you own, you can either scan in the negatives or prints. After scanning photos, you'll often need to do repair work on them, for instance removing scratches or dust particles from the image.

One advantage of scanning photos is that you're not limited by the *image resolution* (in dpi or megapixels) of the camera. However, because images on websites are generally quite small, this isn't a major issue.

Digital photos

Digital photography has come on, in leaps and bounds, in the last few years. Most people now own at least one digital camera, even if it's just the one on their cell phone.

Compared with traditional photos, digital photos are quick, cheap and easy to work with. However, there are some drawbacks.

Digital cameras tend to be significantly more expensive than an equivalent traditional camera. If you've got a really cheap digital camera (under $100), it's likely the pictures it produces won't be that great.

If you're just taking head and shoulders photos of your boss then a mid-range digital camera will do fine.

However, don't expect to be able to take good photos of your range of gold and silver jewelry, unless you've got a very good digital camera and a lot of experience.

Hot tip

For tips on how to take great photos with a digital camera, why not read **101 Digital Photo Tips in easy steps?**

Other people's photography

If you're not a naturally gifted photographer, you might not want to take photos. In some cases, it may not even be practical (could you take a photo of the Earth from space?)

However, if you're not going to take the photos yourself, what can you do? Well, there are a couple of options:

Hire a photographer

Paying a professional photographer to take photos for your site might be a really good investment, especially if you're trying to sell something on it.

The photos for this jeweller's online shop are stunning but cost less than $100*. If just two or three people are tempted by the jewelry after seeing the photos, they'll have paid for themselves.

Use stock photography

Another option, if you're looking for images for your site, is to buy *stock photographs* from an *image library* like **corbis.com** or **gettyimages.com**

These image libraries contain literally millions of photos on every conceivable subject, so you're almost certainly going to be able to find one that suits your needs. They work like a search engine, allowing you to type in keywords and then showing you all the photos that match your search. The screen shot on the right shows the results of a search on Corbis for "British Virgin Islands".

Most professional designers rely a lot on stock photography in their designs, as they can search through the image libraries to find an image that's just right.

Beware

It might be tempting to take photos off the Internet but, unless you've got permission, it's illegal.

If you get caught, you could face anything from an angry email to a court case.

*Thanks to Simon Green, simongreenphotography.co.uk

Photography on a budget

If you've got little or no money to spend on photography and you don't have a digital camera (or don't feel you've got the talent to use it), then don't despair. You've still got plenty of options.

Find a photography student
Most universities and many high schools run photography classes. Contact the tutor to see if any students will take photos for your site, in order to gain experience and develop their portfolios.

Use a budget stock library
The big stock libraries charge anywhere between $50 and several hundred dollars for their photos. But there are several sites that sell high-quality photos for as little as $1 each.

One of the biggest of these is **istockphoto.com** which has a library of over half-a-million photos. Other good sites include **dreamstime.com** and **stockxpert.com**

This photo of a piggy bank cost just $2 from **istockphoto.com**

Free photos
There are even places you can get free photos, many of which are of an acceptable quality.

Stock.xchng (**http://www.sxc.hu**) looks like a normal stock library, but all the images are free. Other sites include **freefoto.com, yotophoto.com** and **morguefile.com**. Perhaps surprisingly, NASA also offer free space-related images on their multimedia site (**http://nix.larc.nasa.gov**).

Istockphoto.com and **dreamstime.com** even offer their members free images every week.

Using thumbnails

The larger a photo is, the longer it takes to load in your web browser. This is obviously a problem if you want your visitors to be able to look through a series of high-quality photos.

Thumbnail images are small versions of larger images, which are quick to download. They allow you to look through a series of photos quickly, before deciding which to view in more detail.

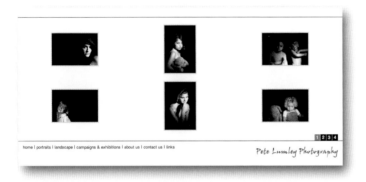

Hot tip

You can use your graphics software to create thumbnails.

However, if you've got a large batch of images to convert to thumbnails, it might be easier to use a specialized program, like Extreme Thumbnail Generator from **exisoftware.com**

When you click on a thumbnail it will usually open up a higher-resolution version of the image, either in the same window (as in this screenshot from **www.petelumleyphotography.com**) or in a pop-up window.

For accessibility reasons, it's usually better to avoid opening new windows, if possible. If you do it, warn the listener by saying "opens in new window", in the link text.

Illustrations & icons

Many people don't think of illustrations as an option for websites, perhaps because they don't think of themselves as illustrators.

Of course, if you are a talented illustrator it helps – but even if you can't draw a circle, you can still use illustrations on your site.

So, what are the options?

If you're not an artist yourself, you've got two options. You can either find an illustrator to create the artwork for you, or buy illustrations from a stock library, just like you would with photos.

Obviously, either option is likely to cost money, but how much will depend on what you require. The advantage of hiring an illustrator is that you can specify exactly what you need. However, it's possible they won't create quite what you'd hoped for, so it's best to pick an illustrator whose style you're happy with.

Many stock photo sites, like **gettyimages.com** or **istockphoto.com**, do illustrations as well. Alternatively, sites like **stockart.com** or **illustrationworks.com** specialize in stock illustrations.

86

sarahhorne.co.uk

These weather icons are part of a set from **iconbuffet.com**

Using icons

Icons can provide valuable visual clues to the meaning of text and links within a website. Like illustrations, they can be created from scratch or bought in from sites like **iconbuffet.com**

As a general rule, icons on the Web should be used to support text, not on their own. In software, people expect to have to learn what icons mean, but people are unlikely to visit your website every day, so it's not reasonable to expect them to learn your icons.

Jpegs & gifs

Images on the Web are almost always saved in one of two file formats, jpeg or gif. You can save any image in either format, using Photoshop, but each has its own strengths and weaknesses.

Jpegs

Jpegs (pronounced j-pegs) can show over 16 million colors, so they're great for photos. Due to the way jpegs store information, they produce a blur around hard edges, so it's better to use gifs for more intricate images containing text or icons.

Gifs

Gifs (pronounced similar to gifts – not jifs) are ideal for saving images with a small number of colors that need to look crisp.

Gifs can only use a maximum of 256 colors, so they're not great for saving photos. However, because they produce sharp images they're ideal for small graphics, with two or three main colors or for images containing text, such as logos or buttons.

Transparent gifs

Gifs can have transparent areas, which let the background color or image show through. This makes them ideal wherever the background might vary and means you can make changes to the site's color scheme without any trouble.

Animated gifs

Animated gifs are made up of a series of images joined together to form a short animation. Used thoughtfully, they can spice up a website or draw attention to important elements on the page.

Seeing a close-up of the same image, as a jpeg (above) and a gif, shows the difference between the two formats.

The gif has less colors giving it a "pixelated" effect, while the jpeg has some distortion around the edges.

	Jpegs	Gifs
Maximum colors	16.7 million	265
File extension	.jpg	.gif
Transparency	No	Yes
Animation	No	Yes
Good for	Photos or gradients	Small images, text, short animations or transparent images
Bad for	Small images or text	Photos or gradients
Use for	Photos	Most other things
Compression	Fractal	Color restriction
Resolution (for web)	72dpi	72dpi

Keeping files small

Have you ever visited a website only to give up after 30 seconds because the page hadn't downloaded yet? Unless you've only just started using the Internet, the answer's almost certainly yes.

But why do some sites take forever to load? One reason is that the *file size* of the images is too large.

File size vs. physical size
Don't confuse the file size of an image with its physical size.

The physical size is how much space your image takes up on the screen – its dimensions. A typical image on a website might be 20mm wide and 30mm high.

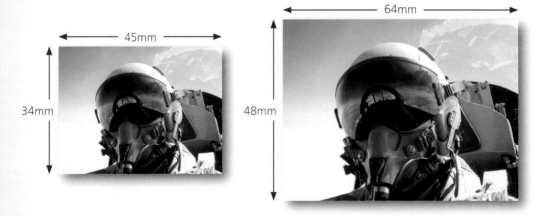

The file size of an image, on the other hand, is how much *information* it takes to store it. In other words how much space it takes up on your hard drive. An image with a larger file size will take longer to download, especially if you don't have broadband.

Two images with the same physical size can have a very different file size, depending on how complex the image is and what *quality* it has been saved at.

Can you make your images download quicker?
Yes. In fact, it's quite easy. Both jpegs and gifs can be *compressed* so they are quicker to download. Compressing an image does mean it loses some quality, so you have to decide how much quality you're prepared to sacrifice for a quicker site.

Your graphics software, like Photoshop, should have a "save for web" option which allows you to save compressed web-ready images. You can also use a stand-alone image optimizer program.

Colorizing a photo

One way of ensuring your photos have a consistent look is to colorize them in a graphics program like Photoshop.

Colorizing a photo basically involves turning it into a black and white photo and then adding a tint. Colorizing can give photos which previously looked quite different a similar appearance.

How do I colorize a photo?
How you colorize a photo depends on which graphics package you're using and there may, in fact, be several ways to do it.

However, it's usually very easy to do. In Photoshop, for example, you press CTRL + U (or ⌘ + U for Mac users), tick "colorize" and then move the sliders until you find a color you like.

By matching the color of your photos to other design elements, like text or background colors, you can create a unified, professional look. Notice how the color of the photo in the design, on the right, matches the navigation, first heading and part of the logo.

Writing useful ALT text

Millions of people around the world have disabilities that make it hard to use badly produced websites. People who are blind, for example, use special software called a *screen reader* to listen to a web page. They sometimes find it impossible to use image-heavy websites, unless a text-only alternative is provided for them.

In most countries, including America, Britain and Australia, there are now laws making it illegal to discriminate against disabled people – and that includes producing websites they can't access.

Accessibility is the practice of making websites as easy to use as possible for people with disabilities.

But I want my site to look good!

Actually, it's fairly easy to make your website accessible and it shouldn't affect the look-and-feel of the site at all. One of the main things you can do is provide alternate text, or ALT text, which anyone who can't see your images will be able to read or hear. You can add ALT text using most web design software, or you can edit the HTML directly.

```
<img src="buffy.jpg" alt="My puppy Buffy" />
```

When you're writing your ALT text you should include enough information so the blind person can work out the subject of the photo, but you're not trying to give a complete description.

For the photo above, "Buffy" wouldn't be enough information, as the listener might think it was a photo of the TV character *Buffy the Vampire Slayer*.

However, "My cute little bichon frise puppy Buffy, sitting on a blue and cream patterned blanket," would be too much information. The ALT text used, "My puppy Buffy," gives just the right amount of information to the listener.

Hot tip

ALT text doesn't just help blind people, it helps Google too.

Because search engines are computer programs, they can't see images.

So, if you use lots of images you're not going to get a good ranking on Google – unless you use ALT text on your images.

Background images

A background image does exactly what you'd expect. It's an image that goes in the background of a web page (or part of one), allowing you to place text and other images on top of it.

Background images can be applied to the whole page or to individual elements on the page, like a heading or link, using css.

This site (**http://rose.clanretribution.net**) looks quite different without the background images

When should you use background images?

Background images are incredibly useful for web designers, especially those who are interested in creating accessible sites using web standards techniques.

Ideally, you should code any image which is purely decorative as a background image, using css. Only images which are an essential part of the content of the page should be coded into the HTML as foreground images (using the `<img … />` tag).

For example, in this furniture maker's site (right), the photo of the dining table and chairs adds useful information about the product, so it should be a foreground image. By contrast, the illustration of the carpenter and the green gradient at the top are only there because they look nice, not to add any useful information or context to the page.

Themed images

It's important to make sure your site looks consistent throughout. One way you can achieve this consistency is to choose a theme for the images you use on your site.

For example, you could choose close-up photos of people's faces to go on your recruitment site or illustrations of cuddly toys, if you were designing a website for a crèche.

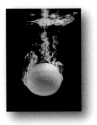  

You don't have to limit your theme to the subject of the images. You can also choose photos that have something visual in common. For example, you could choose photos that were all navy blue, all extreme close-ups or ones that were all blurred.

For **ineasysteps.com**, we chose different themes for different sections of the site.

For the "books" section, all the images are based on the *In Easy Steps* cover design. The "explore the series" section has photos of objects on a colored background.

7 Links and navigation

People interact with websites by clicking on links. This chapter will give you the knowledge you need in order to design a site with easy to use links and navigation.

Linking to other web pages

Links are the oxygen of the Web. Without them, there would be no way to find web pages which you didn't already know existed.

Links are a bit like references in history books or academic papers. They're a way of telling the reader, "Here's some more information on [cats]." You can link to other pages in your own site or to pages from other sites.

What does a link look like?

In practical terms, you probably already know what a link is. It's an area of a web page that takes you to another web page (or part of the same page) when you click on it.

1 Links in text are normally a different color and are underlined. They'll often change when you hold your mouse pointer over them, as seen on the "Web Standards Group" link.

2 In navigation, links aren't usually underlined, but they may be styled (using css) to look like buttons.

3 If you have several links which are related, it makes sense to put them into an unordered list (bullet points).

Links can be text or images. Text links are usually <u>underlined and a different color</u> from the surrounding text. They often change color or show a different image when you move your mouse pointer over them. It's possible to control what they look like, using css, although you should be careful about overdoing this, as it's easy to confuse your visitors.

How do links work?

Links are one of the simplest HTML tags to use. Here's an example of one:

```
<a href="http://www.cheese.com">Cheese!</a>
```

There are basically two parts to a link. The `<a>` and `</a>` tags tell the browser where the link starts and ends*. The `href=""` attribute tells the browser where the link should point to.

*If you're interested, the "a" in the `<a>` tag stands for Anchor and `href` stands for "hypertext reference".

Linking to an email address

If you're setting up a website for your business, you probably want to receive inquiries from potential customers. Adding a link to your email address is the simplest way to allow people to contact you and is really easy to implement.

Any web design program should let you add an email address to your page. You could also write the HTML yourself, using an `<a>` tag, just like you would with a normal link. Rather than linking to a web address, you link to the email address, with the letters `mailto:` in front of it, so the browser can tell it's an email, e.g.

```
<a href="mailto:big@bird.com">big@bird.com</a>
```

Hiding your email address from spammers

One downside to publishing your email address on your website is that you could get more *spam* (unsolicited emails) as a result.

People who send spam usually write special programs, called *spambots*, to scour the Web, looking for email addresses to add to their databases. There are, however, several ways to protect yourself from getting added to spammers' databases.

For example, you could include your email address on the page using Javascript, rather than plain HTML. Spambots can't normally understand Javascript, so they won't see your email. However, although this method is effective, it means people with Javascript turned off won't be able to contact you.

A better way is to encode your email using special HTML codes, rather than using the @ symbol or the **.com** or **.co.uk** extensions, which spambots look for in order to recognize emails. Rather than writing `bill.gates@microsoft.com` in the HTML, you would write `bill&#046;gates&#064;microsoft&#046;com`

Including a contact form as well

Don't forget, not everyone has an email program, like Outlook Express, set up on the computer they're using to surf the Web.

For example, if somebody's looking at your site from a friend's computer or in a library, they won't have email set up. So, it's important to give people another way to get in touch, such as a contact form. Setting one up is fairly easy (see page 109).

Adding image links

Websites would look pretty dull without images. One very common use for them is as links and in navigation.

There are two ways to turn images into links. You can either put a normal image (`<img ... />` tag) inside a link (`<a>`), or you can add a background image to the link itself, using css. Although either method works, it's probably better to use css, as it's easier to make changes, more accessible to people with disabilities and better for your performance in Google.

The arrow images on this page from **pluiplui.com** are links*

Mouseovers

You may have seen buttons or images on a website that change when you move your mouse pointer over them. These are called *image rollovers* or *mouseovers*.

Mouseovers are a useful way of indicating visually which link your mouse pointer is over, as well as being quite attractive.

Mousovers can be done using Javascript, but the best way to create them is with css, using the `:hover` pseudo-class. The trick is to have a background image on the link and then change the image when someone hovers over it. For example:

```
a {
    background-image: url(button.gif);
}

a:hover {
    background-image: url(button-on.gif);
}
```

Hot tip

For more information about using css to create image rollovers, read **css in easy steps**.

*Thanks to Joern Bargmann at **biconcav.com** and Wiebke von Ahn for the screenshot.

Adding a navigation bar

If you've got more than a single page on your website, it's essential to give people a way to navigate it.

Most sites have a *navigation bar* (or *menu*) along the top of the page, or down the left-hand side. Unless you've got a very, very good reason, you should too. If you put your navigation in an unexpected position, people will need to spend time working out how to navigate the site, rather than looking at the content.

It's also important that the navigation looks consistent across the site. If one section looks different from the others, people can become disorientated and think they've left the site.

456bereastreet.com has clean, attractive and easy to use navigation

The 7 link rule

People find choosing between more than about 7 links at a time difficult, so it usually takes longer and requires more thought.

If you do have more than 7 pages in your site, you'll need to group them into sections or put some of the less important ones in a secondary navigation bar at the bottom of the page. If there are more than 7 sections in your site, consider grouping some together into sub-sections.

As a general rule, you should try to avoid giving people more than 7 choices at any stage while they're on your site. Otherwise you're making things more difficult than they need to be.

Why be conventional?

Sometimes, designers get carried away with being different just for the sake of it. A good web designer should try to create an attractive, usable site that meets the site owner's goals, rather than trying to impress people with their "creativity".

The worst example of designers being different for the sake of it is *mystery meat navigation* (MMN)*. MMN is the name given to navigation that is unconventional and difficult to use, usually because no words are displayed until you move your mouse pointer over a link (that you may not even know is there).

It's obvious when you think about it, that navigation is for one thing and one thing only–navigating. Having navigation people can't understand is like having a blank road sign–pointless.

Conventions serve a useful purpose in web design. Remember, web design's not graphic design, it's much more like product design. Websites have to be used, not just looked at. Cell phone designers put numbers on the keys, rather than abstract symbols. Why? Because a phone without numbers would be unusable.

People look for a list of links along the top or at the left. If the navigation's not there, they'll get confused. If there's nothing but a few meaningless symbols on the page, they'll probably just leave.

Keep links underlined

On the Web, underlined text indicates a link. Sometimes it's tempting to remove it, using CSS, so the page looks better. Don't. If links aren't underlined, a lot of people won't realize they're links. However, it's OK to remove the underline in places like the navigation, where people expect links.

Visited links should look different

It's important for people to be able to tell which pages they've already visited. Normally, visited links are a different color from unvisited links and it's a good idea to stick to this convention. However, there are other ways to indicate visited links, such as putting a check mark afterward (which can be done with CSS).

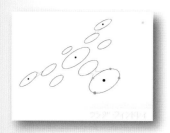

This site may look nice, but where do you click to get to the next page?

98

*For an explanation of the term "Mystery Meat Navigation", visit **webpagesthatsuck.com**

extremely popular hitting the front page of digg.com ✔ and t of my web design agency. In short it was a useful marketing

Navigation on large sites

These days, sites with hundreds, thousands or even millions of pages are becoming more and more common. The BBC website, for example, has over 20 million pages, according to Google.

It's obviously not possible to have a navigation bar with 20 million links. So, how can you design a site that allows people to access all your pages, but is still easy to use?

The first thing to realize is that there isn't a single correct way to design navigation for a large site. There are several different strategies you can use*, including *drop down menus*, *flyout menus*, *expanding menus* and *tag-based navigation*. Visit other large sites, like **bbc.co.uk**, **cnn.com** and **bn.com**, to see how they approach it.

Which navigation strategy you use depends on the site, your target audience, the look-and-feel you want to achieve and your own personal preferences.

It's important with large sites to try several different approaches to navigation and then do some *wireframe user testing*, with a selection of real people in your target audience (see page 129). The approach your visitors find easiest to use is the right one.

1   **Homeoffice.gov. uk** has over 15,000 pages, so a good site search function is essential.

2   There are three levels of navigation on the Home Office site. When you click on a section, like "Security", the next level of navigation is revealed.

This is a very elegant way of dealing with the problem of navigating a large site like this.

3   A "related links" section helps people to find other pages that might interest them.

4   People who can't find exactly what they're looking for in the navigation, are reminded about the advanced search.

*Unfortunately, there isn't space in this book to cover all of them. However you could search Google for more information.

Using a drop-down menu

If your site has more than a handful of pages, you'll need to split them into sections, so you don't overwhelm your visitors.

However, this does mean you have to think carefully about your navigation bar. You need to decide how to allow your visitors to get to each page within your site, without being given too many choices in one go.

One neat solution is to use a *drop-down menu*. These are like a normal menu, except when you move your mouse pointer over one of the links, a sub-menu is revealed underneath, with links to additional pages.

Drop-down menus are useful if you need people to be able to access every single page of the site from a single navigation bar.

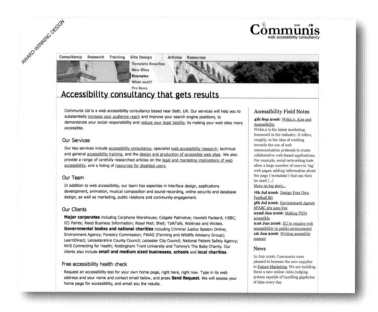

How to make a drop-down menu

Drop-down menus used to be made using Javascript or DHTML. Although this method works, it's very complicated to set up, is inaccessible to many disabled people and doesn't help your performance in Google either.

A much better way to create drop-down menus is to use a css-based, web standards technique, like *suckerfish drop-downs*, **http://alistapart.com/articles/dropdowns/**

Breadcrumb trails

On large websites, it's easy to forget where you are within the site. Some people will become disorientated once they've clicked on more than a few links, which as a web designer or website owner isn't something you want to happen.

One of the most common ways to show your visitors where they are, within your site, is to use a *breadcrumb trail*. The term comes from the fairy tale, Hansel and Gretel. In the story, Hansel left a trail of breadcrumbs in the woods, so he and his sister could find their way back home*.

1 The breadcrumb trail on the In Easy Steps website helps people work out where they are within it.

Likewise, a breadcrumb trail is a list of links which helps visitors to your site retrace their steps. Usually, a breadcrumb trail is a horizontal list of links, which shows visitors where they are within the site.

*In the fairy tale, the crumbs were eaten by birds, leaving the children stranded in the woods. Luckily, on a website, breadcrumb trails are a much more successful strategy for retracing your steps.

For example, in the page shown above, the breadcrumb trail reads:
Home > Books > Getting Noticed on Google in easy steps.

Normally, a breadcrumb trail shows where the visitors are within the overall site. However, it's also possible to show the last few pages your visitor had looked at.

Adding a site search

What's the first thing people will do when they visit your site? Around half of them will probably look for a search box of some kind. Why? Well, perhaps because people are so used to searching. Just think about how often you use Google each day.

So, if you have an easy to use search box on your site, you'll automatically be helping many of your visitors to navigate it.

Where should you put your search?

Most site search boxes are in the top right-hand corner of the page. Putting yours there will help your visitors find it quickly.

The search results page

People often put little or no effort into the way the search results are ordered or the design of the page, concentrating instead on designing the homepage or product pages.

That's a bit like spending lots of money designing a beautiful sign to go outside a shop and then hiring unhelpful staff. You might attract lots of people in, but they'll leave pretty quickly.

Your search results page needs to be well laid out, easy to read and (most importantly) the results need to be relevant to your visitors.

Make sure you clearly highlight the page names and leave enough space between results, for the page to be easily read.

Add an advanced search

If your visitors haven't found what they were looking for straight away, give them the chance to search again, this time for something more specific.

1 Reminding your visitors what they've searched for, helps them decide what to search for next, if they haven't found what they want.

2 Separating each result into its own clearly defined area of the page, makes the search results much more usable.

3 Adding extra information about each link, helps your visitors decide whether it's worth looking at the page.

4 The title of each article is linked, but as it's not underlined some people won't realize. So, a button gives them an alternative way to reach the page.

Adding a sitemap

Some sites only have a few pages, but others have hundreds, thousands or even millions. If you've got that many pages, it's not practical to put links to every single one in your navigation, so most large sites settle for just including links to the main sections and sub-sections of the site.

Having a sitemap helps visitors find their way around quickly and easily, as well as providing a way for them to check if your site has the page they're after. People don't like wasting time, especially online, so if they can check whether or not you have a page about your returns policy or job opportunities, they'll appreciate it.

Sitemaps also help search engines like Google to index your site, especially if it uses inaccessible techniques like DHTML drop-down menus or Flash-based navigation.

1 For a sitemap to be useful, your visitors need to know it's there.

As you can see from the screenshot on the left, on **ineasysteps.com**, we included an ad for the sitemap at the side of most pages on the site.

On larger sites, you don't necessarily have to link to every single page, as it would be impractical. What's important is to give people an overview of your site and the main sections.

Advertise your sitemap

Sitemaps are only useful if your visitors know they exist. There's no point in creating one and then having a tiny link hidden at the bottom of the page, where nobody ever looks. Put a prominent link to your sitemap on every page, if possible.

Creating a smooth journey

1 This is a transitional page. It only exists so people can choose which page to look at next.

People don't want to spend long on transitional pages, so all the links are clearly labeled and the main ones are large and central.

2 The navigation is clear and runs along the top. There are only 5 choices for the visitor to make.

3 A well positioned search box is vital on a large site.

4 A breadcrumb trail helps people orientate themselves within the website.

5 Giving people alternative ways to get to the same information will make your site easier to use.

6 Pages that don't fit into any of the main sections have links in a secondary navigation bar at the bottom of each page.

Websites aren't just looked at, people interact with them – and one of the main ways they do, is by clicking on links.

If you want your website to achieve its goals, it's vital the site is easy to use. In order to be easy to use, you have to make sure your links and navigation will allow your visitors a smooth journey through the site.

What do your visitors want?

It's important to put yourself in the shoes of your visitors when you design a site. Ask yourself what kind of people they are and what they want to do on your website.

We redesigned the **ineasysteps.com** with a typical *In Easy Steps* reader in mind. After some research, we discovered the main reason people come to the website is to find out about the books and download the exercises and source code which accompany many of the titles in the *In Easy Steps* line.

So, we decided to make the books the focus of the homepage, rather than corporate news or information. As the range of books is large, a list of all the *In Easy Steps* titles would have been long and confusing.

No two people are alike, so we've given our readers a variety of paths through the site, to find books. As well as exploring book categories, like "Internet", "Design" and "Programming", people can jump straight to any title using a select box. We also highlight our newest and best selling books on the homepage and allow people to see thumbnails of all the covers.

8 Web forms

Next to links, forms are the main way people interact with a website. In order for your site to achieve your business goals, it's important your forms are easy to use.

What are web forms?

Online forms are a way for your visitors to send you information. They're very similar to the printed forms you have to fill out when you set up a bank account or apply for a job.

In fact, these days many people actually use websites with online forms to apply for a job or open a bank account.

As with a printed form, your visitor will send you the information on the web form once they've filled it in. However, rather than mailing it, the data is sent electronically over the Internet.

Don't forget

Not all forms are as long as this credit card application.

Some forms, like search forms, just have one field and a submit button.

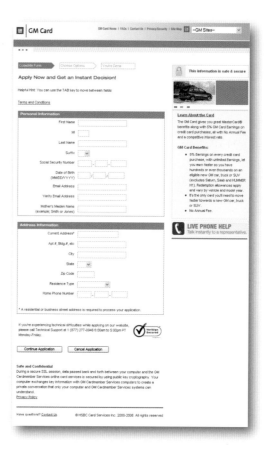

Because it's received electronically, you can do lots of different things with the information you receive from a web form.

For example, you could add it to a database, email it to your company director or even accept money from the customer's credit card or bank account.

How forms work

After you've filled in an online form, you *submit* it by clicking on a submit button. Submitting the form sends the information you've just entered to a computer program on the web server.

The program will usually be written in a server-side programming language like PHP, ASP, Java or ColdFusion. It will often be linked to a database like MYSQL, Access or Oracle.

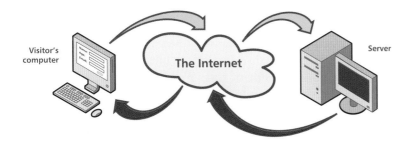

Then what happens?
What happens next depends entirely on what the server-side program has been created to do. For instance, the program could:

- Send you an email
- Add your contact information to a database
- Show you a list of shoes in your size
- Work out your mortgage payments for the next 30 years
- Book you into a hotel
- Show you a list of train times
- Charge your credit card to pay for the book you just ordered

Creating pages on-the-fly
After it's completed its task, the server-side program will usually create a web page and send it back to you. This might simply be a page saying, "Thanks for filling out our contact form."

However, often the program will create a one-off web page specifically for you, based on the information you filled in.

For example, if you use the search form on Google's homepage, it compiles a list of relevant websites and puts the first ten of them on its results page. This page didn't exist before you filled in the form and was created while you were waiting.

Basic form elements

Forms are made up of *fields,* which you can enter information into and, a *submit button* that sends the information to the server.

Text boxes

There are several types of fields, but the most common is a *text box.* Visitors to your site type information directly into a text box, for example, their name, email address or phone number.

Password boxes, text areas and file uploads

Password boxes are similar to text boxes, but hide the information you type on screen (usually using stars), to protect your password.

Text areas are also similar to text boxes, but they let the visitor submit more than one line of text. *File upload fields* let people upload files to your server.

Select boxes (drop downs)

Select boxes allow you to restrict the options a visitor has when filling out the form. For instance, if you ask for someone's gender, you can restrict the answer to "male" or "female".

Radio buttons and check boxes

Another way of restricting the answers people can give, is to use a check box or radio button. Check boxes and radio buttons look fairly similar, but they work slightly differently. You can only select one radio button out of a set, but use as many check boxes as needed.

Submit buttons

When the form is complete, your visitors need to click on a *submit button* to send the information.

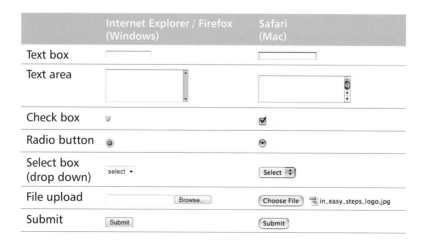

	Internet Explorer / Firefox (Windows)	Safari (Mac)
Text box		
Text area		
Check box	☑	☑
Radio button	◉	◉
Select box (drop down)	select ▾	Select ⬍
File upload	Browse...	Choose File in_easy_steps_logo.jpg
Submit	Submit	Submit

Adding a contact form

You might think a website would mean you'd have less contact with members of the public, but nothing could be less true.

If your website's doing its job properly, lots of people will want to contact you. People will want to ask questions, request quotes and place orders. If you're lucky, some might even want to tell you how much they enjoyed using your site.

Don't forget

Not everyone will want to get in touch with you using your contact form.

People will appreciate it if you give them the choice of how to contact you, so include your phone number, email address and postal address too.

109

What happens once you submit the form?
In the case of a contact form, the details are usually formatted and then emailed to the website owner. The person who submitted the form is then taken to a "thank you" page.

It's also possible to add some of the information to a database. For example, you might add the name and email address to your mailing list database. Make sure you let people know you're going to do this though and give them the chance of opting out.

One advantage of having a contact form, compared with just providing your email address, is that you can ask people for specific information to help you deal effectively with their inquiry.

A real estate agent, for example, might ask you whether you were a potential tenant, landlord, home buyer or seller. Your message could then be forwarded automatically to the right department.

Error checking

People make mistakes when they complete forms, for example, they might put information in the wrong place or miss some required fields.

Luckily, with a web form you can help point out their mistakes.

Using Javascript

The simplest way to check if the form has been filled out correctly is to use Javascript.

When somebody fills out a form and hits the submit button, Javascript will check the form to see if the fields have been filled out correctly. If they have then the form will get submitted, as normal, but if any mistakes have been made a pop-up window will appear, warning them.

The disadvantage of using Javascript to check a form is that if your visitor isn't able to use Javascript, the form won't get checked.

Using a server-side program

The alternative to using Javascript to check your forms is to check them using a server-side programming language, like PHP or ASP.

In this case, somebody would fill out a form and then submit it, sending the information to the server.

A program on the server would then check the information, for example, it could check to see if all the required fields had been filled and that the email address was valid.

If the information was OK, the program would then send the visitor to the next part of the process, like the "thank you" page. However, if there was a mistake, the program would send the visitor back to the form, pointing out what the mistakes were.

Which method should you use?

The advantage of server-side error checking is that the visitor doesn't need Javascript. However, it's also slower as they have to download a whole page just to find out they've missed their email.

Because of this, many sites use both Javascript and server-side error checking, as it's quicker for the majority of visitors with Javascript, but still works for those who don't have it.

Hot tip

To find out how to check forms for errors using PHP, why not read **PHP 5 in easy steps?**

110

Beware

Don't make every field required. The harder you make it for people to fill in a form, the less people will complete it.

Designing easy to use forms

Forms are not the "sexiest" aspect of web design, but they're easily one of the most important, especially for commercial sites.

Perhaps the two most common types of form are:

- Contact forms
- Order forms for online shops (and other ecommerce sites)

If people can't use the forms on your website, they'll leave and you'll lose their business. It's that simple. So you need to give a lot of thought to the design of your forms and you need to get real people to test them.

Less is more (yet again)

The longer a form is, the less likely people are to complete it. It's vital that you ask as few questions on a form as possible.

Never ask marketing questions

If somebody is about to buy something from you then make it easy for them. Don't, under any circumstances, lose a sale by asking them a series of pointless marketing questions.

1. If you need to get lots of information from your customers, then splitting the form up into several pages should make people much more likely to complete the process.

2. Giving your customers an indication of how many steps there are means they're less likely to give up half-way.

3. You should break down long forms into clearly labeled sections, as it makes them seem less daunting.

4. Only use required fields where you really do require the information. Asking an investor for their full address is fine when they're signing up for an account.

   If it was just an inquiry about your restaurant's opening hours, however, then you wouldn't need this information.

Forms: top design tips

1 **Keep the number of fields to a minimum**

The longer your forms are, the less likely it is that people will complete them. Don't ask unnecessary questions, or you risk losing a potential sale.

2 **Select required fields carefully**

If somebody's just filled in a long form, they'll be disappointed (and likely to just quit) if they're presented with an error message because they didn't fill in their fax number or third address line. Only make a field required if you absolutely need the information.

Hot tip

For more tips on designing online forms that are easy to use, visit: **http://alistapart.com/ articles/sensibleforms/**

3 **Be flexible**

If somebody wants to put brackets around the area code in their phone number, or separate their credit card number into 4 digit chunks, then let them. A good programmer should find it easy to process the information before it goes into a database, in order to make it consistent.

4 **Split long forms into separate sections**

Long forms are daunting. Splitting them into clear sections makes them seem less frightening to your visitors.

5 **Have a page count**

Sometimes it's best to split very long forms into several pages. If you do this, make sure you give your visitors a clear indication of how many more pages they have left to complete.

6 **Use plain English in your error messages**

If somebody makes a mistake or leaves some information out, tell them in plain language what they've done wrong and how to fix the problem. Highlighting the fields they need to look at (in red with a short message) will simplify the process for them.

7 **Get real people to test your forms**

Even if you don't test any other aspect of your site, it's vital to get potential customers to test your forms. See page 129 for more information about user testing.

9 Making your site sticky

What is stickiness? It's what web designers call a site's ability to keep visitors coming back.

Why do people return to websites?

It's relatively easy to get people to come to your site. However, it's much harder to get them to stay on it for a long time and then to come back repeatedly.

Web designers call a site that's able to keep visitors and attract them back, "sticky".

If you want your site to be sticky (and you should), you need features that your target audience will want to use repeatedly.

Pages that aren't sticky

Most business websites have pages with names like "home", "about us", "our products" and "contact us". Having pages like these makes a lot of sense as people like straightforward, easy to understand content. However, if that's all you've got on the site, don't expect them to come back often. After all, would you?

What makes a site sticky?

That depends on your target audience. If your site is aimed at teenagers, then games, contests and mobile phone ringtones, might entice them back. If you're aiming at retired professionals, you'll need to take a different approach.

The main thing, whatever your site, is to try to think from your target audience's point of view. Better yet, ask them. What problems do they face? What have they come to your website looking to do? Is there anything that would make them return *even if they didn't want to buy something*?

If your site offers them something useful or entertaining, they're much more likely to come back than if you've just got an online shop like all your competitors.

Perhaps your site sells video games and consoles. You've got an easy to use online shop and great prices, but what if you had a database of tips and cheats for all your games? Gamers would visit your site to get cheat codes even if they didn't want to buy a game, but when they *did* want to buy one, who would they turn to?

Something for nothing

People love a freebie. One of the best ways to get people to return to a site regularly is to give them something for nothing, or the chance to get something for nothing.

Many stock photography sites, like **istockphoto.com**, let registered members download a free photo every week. This costs the site virtually nothing, but it means people come back regularly, so when they do need to buy a photo, they're more likely to choose that site over another one.

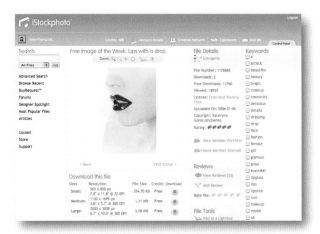

If your site sells something physical, like books or CDs, it's not feasible to give everyone a free copy. However, you could offer sample chapters (or tracks) or give visitors the chance to win one of your products in a contest.

Give your visitors something useful

Of course, you don't have to resort to bribery to get people to return to your site. Why not offer your visitors a tool, tutorial or some information they might find useful?

A scuba diving center could offer visitors maps of local dive sites; while a hardware store might let its customers download project fact sheets like, "How to put up a shelf," or "How to rewire a plug."

When you offer your visitors a freebie, it's a good opportunity to ask them for their email address, so you can contact them when you update your site or add more free content. Make sure you ask their permission first.

Ineasysteps.com has a database of articles by our authors, which visitors to the site can download for free.

Adding news

If your site stays the same, week in week out, people are unlikely to visit it more than a few times. Once they've read everything, why would they want to return.

So, if you want people to keep coming back, you need to offer them something new each time. A regularly updated news page not only gives your visitors new content, but it also reassures them the site is up to date.

If you run a business, you might want to mix company news with more general industry news, so your stories don't sound boastful.

 If you see the RSS icon on a web page, then it has an RSS feed. Adding an RSS feed is a great way to get people to come back to your site on a regular basis.

116

Add an RSS news feed

If you use the Web lots, you may have seen the RSS icon ( ).

Rss stands for *Really Simple Syndication*. It's an easy way for people to access their favorite content without having to download the unnecessary parts of a web page, like images or navigation.

To use RSS you need a program called an *aggregator*. Some browsers (like Firefox) let you read RSS feeds or you can download a special program like Feed Demon (**feeddemon.com**).

Many sites now offer an RSS feed of their news pages, as it encourages people to come back to sites they like. Setting up an RSS feed isn't hard, but you might need to do some coding. For more information, search Google for "Setting up an RSS feed."

Installing a message board

Message boards are a fantastic way to get people to return to your site day after day. Not only are members of your message board community likely to use the rest of your site, but other people are more likely to stumble across it through Google.

Aren't message boards just for kids?

Message boards aren't right for every site, but it's certainly not just bored teenagers who use them.

Message boards work well where there's a community of people with a common interest who want to share ideas, ask questions or just chat. The common interest can be anything, from an admiration for a pop star to an interest in second-hand Fords.

Message boards are also a good way to promote the expertise of your business, as well as helping potential customers through an "ask the experts" section.

Beware

Anyone can post on a message board but they might not have the best interests of your business at heart.

Having moderators, who can edit or delete people's posts, is essential. You can also set the software up to delete certain words, like swear words.

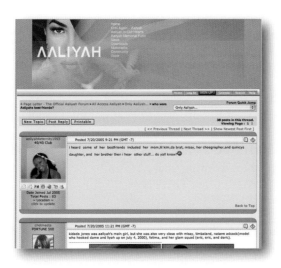

Entertainment sites, like **aaliyah.com**, often have very busy message boards

Can anyone set up a message board?

Starting a message board is a lot easier and less expensive than you might expect. In fact, there are several free message boards available like Vanilla (**getvanilla.com**) or ASP DEV (**asp-dev.com**).

To run a message board, your server will need to support a programming language (like PHP or ASP) and a database (like MYSQL or Access) but the installation process should be fairly easy.

Games & contests

The Internet is full of ways to waste time. However, if people are going to waste time, don't you want them to do it on *your* site?

Games

As any parent will tell you, computer games can be highly addictive. If you've got a good game on your site, you'll find visitors coming back again and again. And again. And again.

Of course, people won't get addicted to just any game, you need to do something quirky or original. People are unlikely to be impressed by a "health and safety crossword" or yet another version of Tetris.

Online games don't come cheap. Most use Flash (though some use DHTML, Java or Shockwave) and require fairly advanced programming skills, as well as high-quality design and illustration. So, unless you're exceptionally talented, you'll probably have to hire a web design company that has experience of online games.

However, if you've got the resources, online games are a powerful way to increase traffic and make your site stickier.

Contests

Some people spend hours at a time searching Google for contests. There are even websites dedicated to providing lists of online contests. So, they're a great way to attract visitors to your website and to keep them coming back.

Of course, not everyone who finds your site through a contest will come back and explore it, but even if a small percentage do, it will have been worth your while.

If you want people to come back to your site, it's important to run regular contests and let your visitors know when to come back. You can also ask them for their email address, so you can contact them when your next contest starts.

10 Building your website

So, you've planned your website, decided on a look-and-feel and written all the copy – but how do you go about actually creating a website? This chapter will take you through the process of building a typical website.

The web designer's toolbox

As with any job, you need certain tools to be a web designer.

Physical equipment
It's fairly obvious, but if you want to design websites you're going to need a computer that's connected to the Internet.

More than 9 out of 10 people who use the Web have a Windows PC, so most web designers choose to work on one. However, it's fine to use an Apple Mac, provided you have a PC to test sites on.

Graphics software
If you want any pictures on your site, you're going to need to invest in some graphics software. The most common one for web design is Adobe Photoshop, but there are many others like Fireworks or Paint Shop Pro.

Web authoring software
Once you've decided what your site is going to look like, you'll need to build it using HTML and CSS.

Web authoring software, which you use to write the HTML, comes in two types. Visual tools let you create the page without having to see the code. By contrast, code-based tools let you create the HTML yourself by hand. Dreamweaver is the software of choice for most web designers, as it allows you to create a site visually or using its *code view*.

FTP software
After you've built your site, you'll need to transfer it to your web server using a *File Transfer Protocol* (or FTP) program. Many web authoring programs, like Dreamweaver, have built-in FTP software but there are also several dedicated FTP packages with more advanced functions.

Web browsers
As a web designer, you should download a few web browsers, so you can check how your site will look to all of your visitors.

The most common browser is Internet Explorer, which comes installed on any PC, but you should also download Firefox and Opera. Safari is the standard browser on Macs.

Where do I start?

There's no right or wrong way to design a website. Some people start by writing the content, while others develop the database first and some begin with the HTML.

However, the approach most professional web designers take is to design the site first (using a graphics tool like Photoshop) and then to code the HTML and CSS, using web standards techniques.

Why design the site before you code it?

This approach has several advantages over other methods. First, it means the person doing the design doesn't necessarily have to do the coding.

People who are good at graphic design and Photoshop, might be weak at HTML or server-side programming and vice-versa, so it makes sense to let people concentrate on their strengths.

On larger websites, it's unrealistic to have the same person doing everything. Even if one person is a brilliant graphic designer, HTML coder, copywriter and PHP programmer, they simply won't have time to do everything.

Also, it's much quicker, easier and cheaper to make changes to a design in Photoshop, rather than once it's coded as HTML, even for an experienced web designer.

It saves time and money if the web designer can create a few possible designs, or *treatments*, in Photoshop for the website owner to choose from, before the designer starts building the site.

You can also show the designs to potential customers, in order to gauge their reactions and discover whether they can find information easily.

Preparation is everything

Before you open Photoshop, or even start sketching designs on a napkin, you should have a clear plan written down for the site.

Know who your target audience is, what you want the site to achieve and what sections and pages you plan to have on it. Once you've done the design in Photoshop, go back to your plan and ask yourself if your design meets the goals you set for the site. If possible, ask other people too–you may not be objective.

Sketching out ideas

The first thing a lot of web designers do before starting a site, is to write down a list of ideas on a piece of paper.

As well as listing all the pages and sections you want your site to contain, it helps to write down a list of the elements which should appear on each page, in order of importance.

Then, you can start sketching basic layouts for your site. Don't worry too much about the details at this stage, the key is to come up with lots of ideas and then refine one or two of your better designs.

Make sure you design your pages so that the important elements are the most noticeable. Some ways to do this include making them larger, putting them in prominent positions and making sure they're more colorful or contrast heavily with less important elements.

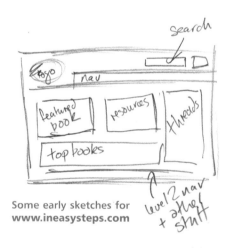

Some early sketches for
www.ineasysteps.com

Is your layout usable?

Like products, websites have to be easy to use, as well as attractive, so it's important to get real people to test your designs.

Larger websites often do *user testing* with *wireframes* of their early designs. A wireframe is a very simple prototype of a web page, showing the basic layout without any of the colors or images that will end up in the final site. Testing how people use wireframes is an excellent way of identifying any usability problems early on, rather than waiting until the site has been launched, when making changes will be harder and more expensive.

Perfecting your design

Once you've sketched your ideas and decided which ones to try out, you're ready to open up Photoshop*.

*Or your chosen graphics software.

Photoshop is the program most web designers use to create the graphics for their sites. Basically, you "draw" your website using Photoshop first, before coding it with HTML and CSS.

One of the big advantages of designing websites this way, is that you can get the design looking exactly how you want it, without having to worry about how to achieve this in HTML.

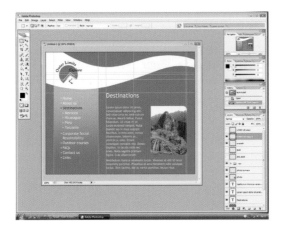

Designs for websites which have been done in Photoshop are called *treatments* or *mockups*. Usually, a web designer will create two or three treatments for a site and then show them to the website owner, who chooses the design he or she likes best. If you're designing a website for yourself, then you could show the treatments to a friend or member of your family.

Often you (or the site owner) will want to make changes to your chosen design, in order to improve it. Most treatments go through several versions before the design is perfected.

It's much easier to make changes to a design in Photoshop than it would be using HTML, so now's the time to finalize the look-and-feel. Making changes will be much harder and more expensive if you leave it until the end of the project.

It's also a good idea to show your design to some potential visitors to gauge their reactions. Why not ask some existing customers to look at your designs?

Don't forget

Once everyone involved in creating the website is happy with the design, it's important to get them to "sign it off".

This means they all sign a document confirming they are happy with it.

Even minor changes can be time consuming and costly, if you wait until after you've written the HTML and completed the server-side programming.

123

Cutting up your design

Websites are coded using HTML, which is a fairly simple computer language, made up of tags. In their simplest form, tags are ways to add extra information to text. For example, you can add an `<h1>` tag to some text if it's the page heading, or you could add an `<a>` tag to some text to turn it into a link.

This was fine in the days when web pages were only created by academics sharing their latest discoveries, but if you're designing a modern website, you probably want it to look attractive.

The blue wireframe diagram (far right) shows the basic structure of the **www.ineasysteps.com** homepage.

Background images are added to the HTML tags using CSS, giving pages a more modern appearance (near right).

124

The way to get web pages to look attractive is to use CSS to *style* the tags in your HTML. For example, you can use CSS to make all the links on the page **bold** or all the sub-headings *purple and italic*.

As well as adding color to text, CSS can add background images to HTML tags. The blue wireframe diagram (above) shows the `<div>` tags on the **ineasysteps.com** homepage. By adding background images to the `<div>` tags, a basic HTML page is turned into an attractive, modern design.

Get the scissors out!

Because web pages are split up into tags, you need to cut your design up into separate images. Then you can attach each image to an HTML tag.

Of course, you don't do this with a pair of scissors, you use Photoshop. There are several ways to do it. You can cut out the images yourself by selecting an area of your design and then copying and pasting it into a new image. Alternatively, you can use Image Ready, a free program which accompanies Photoshop and is designed specifically for cutting up images for websites.

Building your site visually

Once you've completed your designs and cut them up into a series of background images, you're ready to start building the site.

The easiest way to build web pages is to use a visual web authoring program, like Dreamweaver or Microsoft Expression, which creates the HTML and CSS for you automatically. You simply edit the page, just like you would with a Word document.

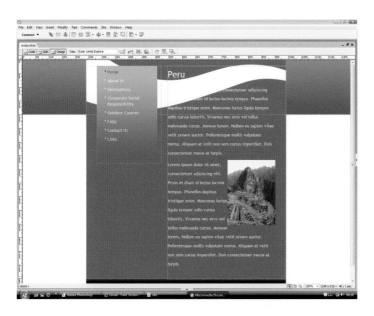

Don't forget

Dreamweaver is really two programs in one.

First there's the "design view" which lets you edit web pages without knowing any HTML.

Then there's the "code view" which lets you code HTML, CSS, Javascript and even PHP.

125

A little knowledge is a dangerous thing

However, unlike Word, it's not a good idea just to pick up a copy of Dreamweaver and start creating pages without any training.

Visual web authoring programs, like Dreamweaver, have a habit of producing very poor-quality HTML code, unless you use them correctly. If you just dive right in and start creating web pages, you'll probably create ones that are slow, inaccessible and struggle to do well in search engines.

It's important to learn the correct way to use your web authoring program, in order to produce a site that uses web standards (HTML, CSS and unobtrusive Javascript).

Don't worry, it's no more complicated to produce a good website, with Dreamweaver, than it is to produce a bad one; you just need to know the tricks of the trade.

Hot tip

For an introduction to designing with web standards using Dreamweaver, visit:
www.sitepoint.com/article/ dreamweaver-8-standards

Building your site by hand

At first, coding the HTML for your site from scratch, without the help of a visual web authoring program, sounds daunting. All of the code is just mumbo jumbo, isn't it?

Actually, learning to code HTML and CSS really isn't all that hard, if you're prepared to put in a little time and effort. Programs like Dreamweaver and Homesite make things a lot simpler, by color-coding your HTML and warning you when you make mistakes.

Why bother learning HTML and CSS?

Using a visual web authoring program is OK while you're starting out, but if you're serious about web design you really should be *hand-coding* your pages.

Visual web authoring programs often produce unnecessarily complex HTML and CSS code, so hand-coded sites tend to be much better.

If you understand the code that lies underneath a web page, you'll also be able to attempt more complicated designs and create cleaner, quicker and more search-engine-friendly code.

Also, if you want to use any server-side programming or databases on your site, you'll need to be able to understand HTML.

Finally, if you ever intend to be a professional web designer, you'll find it much easier to get a job if you can hand-code HTML.

Hot tip

You can check the quality of your HTML code using some software called a *validator*. The official HTML validator is at: **http://validator.w3.org**

Web design on a budget

Professional web design software doesn't come cheap. Photoshop and Dreamweaver will cost you over $1000 combined. Add in a copy of Illustrator & Flash and you're talking about a substantial sum of money.

If you're planning to become a professional web designer, it makes sense to invest in top quality tools like these. However, if you're just designing a site for your club or small business, you could easily spend more money on the software than you would have done hiring an experienced professional web designer.

Don't worry, though, there *are* cheaper alternatives.

Graphics software
Paint Shop Pro (**paintshoppro.com**) is a very powerful graphics package, which many smaller web design companies prefer to Photoshop, partly because it costs less than $100.

GIMPshop (**www.gimpshop.net**) is a free graphics program that works on Windows, Mac and Linux computers. It's modeled on Photoshop, so it's fairly easy to use, but comes without the hefty price tag.

Web authoring software
Because HTML, CSS and Javascript files are basically just text files, you don't actually need any special web authoring software to create web pages, if you know how to hand-code.

Windows comes with a text editor called Notepad, which many professional web designers opt for, as it's free and easy to use. You can find it by clicking on the *start* button (in the bottom left-hand corner) and choosing *all programs* and then *accessories*.

NVU (pronounced N-view) is a free web authoring program which is very similar to Dreamweaver. You can edit web pages visually or manually, using the built-in HTML editor. It has some great features even Dreamweaver doesn't yet have, like built-in support for microformats (see page 136).

FTP software
Like Dreamweaver, NVU has a built-in FTP program. There are also lots of really good free FTP programs like Coffee Cup Free FTP (**www.coffeecup.com/free-ftp**) for Windows or Cyberduck (**www.cyberduck.ch**) for Mac.

Don't forget

Photoshop Elements is a cut-down version of Photoshop, which costs under $100. It's worth considering, especially if you'd like to be a professional web designer one day.

127

Making the back end work

These days, most commercial websites have at least some form of server-side programming.

Even small business sites usually have a basic content management system, which allows the website owner to update the content or even add pages themselves.

Other things that will need server-side programming include contact forms, site wide search engines, blogs and online shops.

What are my options?

If you want your website to run any kind of server-side program, you'll need your server to be set up with a programming language (like PHP) and a database (like MySQL).

The easiest option is to use a program that somebody else has already written. There are a wide variety of existing server-side programs you can use, including content management systems, message boards, online shops and blogging tools.

Some of the better programs cost money, but there are also free, open-source alternatives. You normally have to install the program yourself, which can be a bit tricky. Some web hosting companies give you a set of basic programs (like blogging tools), which you can install on your server through the control panel.

Alternatively, you could create a program yourself from scratch, or hire a professional web developer to do it for you. This will usually give you more control, but will also be more expensive.

Which language should I choose?

If you're going to be doing the programming yourself, PHP is a good first language to learn, as it's easy to understand.

Almost every web host provides PHP free these days and most also let you have MySQL free. There are lots of good books and sites about PHP, as well as scripts you can download and learn from.

If you already know Visual Basic, then ASP is probably your best option, as the code is written in a similar way.

Don't forget

Some common server-side languages include:

- PHP
- ASP
- Java (don't confuse with Javascript)
- ColdFusion
- Ruby on Rails
- ASP .NET
- Perl
- Python

They usually store information in a database like:

- MySQL
- Access
- SQL Server
- Oracle

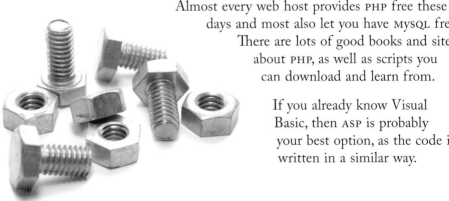

Test early, test often

Unlike posters or brochures, websites are designed to be used. So, it's important to get real people to test your site, in order to identify any usability problems early on.

Remember, your site will be your first point of contact with many customers. If they find the experience slow and frustrating, that's how they're going to think about your company. Do small amounts of testing throughout the web design process. Even on small sites, it's important to do at least a little bit. If you can't afford a full-scale usability test, ask a few friends to look at it. There are several different types of testing you can do, including:

Card sorting

Card sorting is a really useful way to help you decide how to structure your site and, what to call the sections. Write down the name of each page on a card, shuffle them, and ask a few potential customers to sort them into groups and to come up with names for each group. The results can help you decide which sections to have on your site and what to call each one.

Wireframe testing

A *wireframe* is a working prototype of your site (or a section of it), without any colors or images. By asking potential customers to try performing key tasks, you can uncover any usability problems early in the design process. For example, you could ask them to send you an email through your "contact us" page, or you could ask them to buy a digital camera.

Spotting usability problems makes a huge difference to the success of your site. Over half of the people who visit online shops, give up half way through the buying process, often because they found the site difficult to use. Can you afford to let that happen to you?

Design testing

Once you've completed your designs in Photoshop, you can ask potential customers to look at them, for feedback.

Don't ask them if they like the fonts or colors as that's subjective. Instead, ask them to tell you about the page. For example, you could ask questions like, "Are there any contact details on this page?" Ask them to list words that describe the design. If people think your snowboard site is "conservative" and "dull", then perhaps you need to rethink the design.

Beware

The way your customers see your company is often totally different from the way you do.

Creating a "wholesale" and a "retail" section on your site might make sense to you, if that's how you organize your business.

However, if your customers are more interested in finding out about your "computer hardware" and "software packages", then those are the sections to use.

Tables or web standards?

Once upon a time, in the days before electricity, people used candles to light their homes. Candles did the job, but they had many drawbacks. They weren't that bright and they had an annoying tendency to start fires.

When it comes to web design, the equivalent of using a candle to light your office, instead of electricity, is to use *tables* for the layout of your pages, rather than using CSS.

Remind me, what are tables?

Tables are the part of HTML which was designed to be used to display tabular data, like bus timetables or accounts. They're similar to spreadsheets (like Excel) and have columns and rows.

Because HTML was originally designed to display physics papers, rather than to advertise companies, it wasn't built with graphic designers in mind. The first web pages were very simple, with no images or colors and only a few headings breaking up the text.

However, once companies started to get websites, they wanted them to look as attractive as the brochures and posters they were used to. At the time, the only way to create complex, print-like designs was using tables to position images and text on the screen.

This produced horribly complicated HTML code that was slow, inaccessible, hard to update and generally a bit of a mess.

Luckily, a better way to code websites has since been invented. It's called *web standards* and it uses XHTML (the latest version of HTML), CSS and unobtrusive Javascript (or DOM scripting).

Sites built with web standards techniques are faster, more flexible, do better in search engines, are easier to maintain and more accessible to people with disabilities.

They're also much more likely to make your company money and to meet the goals you wrote down when you were planning the website.

So, should I use web standards?

Yes! If you're about to start learning HTML, then make sure you get hold of a book that teaches web standards.

Hot tip

For a great explanation of the benefits of using web standards, go to:
www.boagworld.com/standards

Don't forget

If you already use old-fashioned, table-based techniques to create your sites, you don't have to make the switch to web standards all at once.

Start by learning how to use CSS to style text and add background images, before moving on to more advanced techniques.

Once you've mastered the basics of CSS, you can try doing a simple layout using it.

11 Looking to the future

The Web's constantly evolving, so you need to keep one eye on the future.

The Web (version 2)

When you think about it, you can do some pretty impressive things on the Web. You can buy a book and pay for it with your credit card, or order a last-minute plane ticket and have it shipped directly to your home.

However, the Web was never really designed to do things like this. At its heart, it was designed to help academics share their research, sort of like an electronic library. Just as a library has books full of pages, the Web has sites full of pages.

The problem with web-based applications

Because it's based on pages, the Web is ideally suited to sharing information, but it's slow and awkward when it comes to online applications.

Sending an email using a program on your computer, like Outlook Express, takes a few seconds, but if you use a web-based email service, like Hotmail, it takes much longer as you have to wait for entire web pages to download every time you do something.

Traditionally, online shops (like **amazon. com**) and other web-based applications, require you to go though several pages in order to perform a task.

Web 2.0 applications, on the other hand, work more like programs on your computer.

Reinventing the Web

Wouldn't it be great if web-based applications worked a little more like programs on your computer do? Well, using technologies like AJAX (see page 134), they're starting to.

Rather than having to go through page after page in order to perform a relatively simple task (like buying a book or finding a location on a map), modern web applications, like Gmail and Shopify (often called *Web 2.0* applications), work much more like a normal computer program, allowing you to drag-and-drop content and make changes without having to refresh the entire page.

Of course, there's still a place for traditional websites. Sites that focus on content, like online newspapers, will carry on organizing it into pages for the foreseeable future. However, more and more web-based applications are starting to use AJAX, and other technologies, to behave like everyday computer programs.

Why reinvent the wheel?

One of the most exciting developments in web design, over recent years, has been the introduction of *Application Programming Interfaces*, or APIs for short.

The term API is a very boring name for something surprisingly exciting. Basically, an API is just a way for one computer program to talk to another. This doesn't sound particularly interesting, but it becomes intriguing when you realize the possibilities it creates.

This website (for a web design conference), uses the Google Maps API to show where the delegates live.

Standing on the shoulders of giants

Essentially, APIs allow you to use applications developed by other companies, like Google, Yahoo or Amazon, on your own website, often for free.

For example, Google Maps (**http://maps.google.com**) has an API which allows you to add a map to your site and customize it. Rather than having to write your own map application from scratch, you can simply use Google's and tailor it.

There's also an API for Amazon, which allows you access to its entire product catalogue (not just the books), including all the photos and customer reviews. APIs like this open up a wide range of possibilities for web designers. For example, if you were designing a DVD review website, you could include the average Amazon customer rating alongside the reviewer's own rating.

Hot tip

Sites which put an API to an innovative use are called *mashups*. Some interesting ones using Google Maps include:

- **housingmaps.com**
- **nyccabfare.com**
- **chicagocrime.org/map**

AJAX

the way of the future?

The Web is constantly evolving. Twenty years ago, it didn't even exist. What will it be like twenty years from now? It's impossible to tell, of course, but for a glimpse of what the future holds you could look at some websites that use AJAX.

What is AJAX and why should I care?

AJAX as a way to create websites which work more like the programs that run on your computer.

Traditionally, people interact with websites by clicking on links and submitting forms. Even the slightest change requires an entire page to be downloaded.

With AJAX, this is no longer the case. You can make changes without having to download an entire page (which really speeds things up) and you can even drag-and-drop things, just like you'd expect to be able to do in a program on your PC.

How does AJAX work?

Rather than waiting for an entire web page to be downloaded (including all of the images, CSS and Javascript), AJAX just downloads small pieces of information and then uses Javascript to dynamically update the web page.

This makes for a much quicker and generally more user-friendly experience.

Online shopping system Shopify (**shopify.com**), uses AJAX to make the admin area much quicker and easier to use.

Why is it called AJAX?

The acronym AJAX stands for Asynchronous Javascript and XML. It's not actually a new technology, it's an innovative approach to developing websites.

AJAX uses a set of web technologies that already exist and have been in use for years, including HTML, CSS, unobtrusive Javascript and the XML HTTPRequest object (don't worry if you don't know what this means—it's not important until you start using AJAX).

Which sites use AJAX already?

AJAX is already being used on some very high profile websites, such as Google Maps and Gmail. Other examples include **flickr.com, basecamphq.com** and **shopify.com**

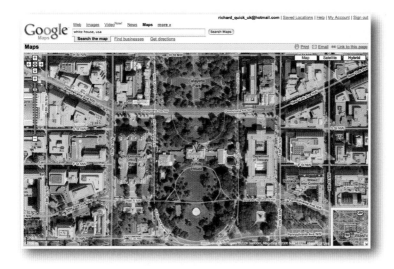

Google Maps is probably the most impressive use of AJAX, so far. Why not visit **http://maps.google.com** to see it in action?

135

Should I use AJAX on my website?

Not necessarily. If your site is mainly based on content, you probably don't need to think about using AJAX just yet. Sites for small businesses, newspapers or universities are unlikely to need to use it.

AJAX is really an approach for developing online applications. If your company has an online shop, or any other type of ecommerce site, it's worth considering using AJAX in order to speed things up for your customers. However, you need to ensure it also works for people who have disabled Javascript.

Mastering microformats

Every web page contains information. Most websites have a contact page, with a phone number, email address and possibly a street address. Others have reviews of products, books or CDs.

Microformats are a way to label certain information, like contact details or reviews, so it can easily be extracted from your web page, by a suitable computer program or website.

Although microformats exist to make it easier for computers to extract information from web pages, they're designed to be easy for people to use. For example, many microformats simply involve adding certain class names to an HTML tag.

Don't forget

There's more information about microformats at **www.microformats.org**

If a web page uses HTML on its own, it's very difficult to write a computer program which can examine the web page, work out what kind of information is on the page and extract it.

For example, look at the following piece of HTML:

```
Clark Kent,
Smallville.
```

How can a computer program work out what kind of information the word "Smallville" is? Is it a town? A country? A type of car?

Obviously, it's going to be pretty difficult. However, using the *hCard* microformat, you can label each piece of information so that it's obvious to a computer what kind of information it is.

```
<div class="vcard">
  <span class="fn">Clark Kent</span>,
  <div class="adr">
   <span class="locality">Smallville</span>.
  </div>
</div>
```

That's basically it! Microformats are just a set of HTML class names and other similarly easy to use attributes.

Why use microformats?

Why not? Once you know about microformats, it's not hard to use them. Like RSS, they provide an easy way for people (and other websites) to access information from your site, increasing the number of visitors you get. They could also prove a useful SEO (search engine optimization) technique in future, as sites spring up to harvest data stored in microformats.

Some organizations already using microformats include:

- Google
- Yahoo
- Apple
- Avon
- Wordpress

12 Business websites

More and more business is being done on the Web. In this chapter, you'll learn how you can use your website to increase your company's profile and reach new markets.

What makes a good business website?

People get into business for a wide variety of reasons. Some do it so that they have more control over their future, some join a family business out of loyalty, others are sick of working for a boss they hate. At the end of the day though, all businesses are about making money—otherwise the owner would have set up a charity.

So the point of a business website should *always* be to help the business make more money—usually either by increasing its revenue or reducing its costs.

Remember the bottom line
It's easy to get over-excited by all the fantastic creative and technical things you can do with a website. You could have streaming video and a funky Flash interface. Perhaps a DHTML drop-down menu and an online database would be better?

Before getting too carried away with the endless possibilities, ask yourself how your site's going to help your business make money. If you're not sure, you probably need to throw everything you've done so far in the trash and start from scratch. A business site that doesn't help the business make money is a bad site.

Have a clear goal and focus on it
When you were planning your website you should have written down a clear goal. For a business site, if you manage to achieve your goal, then your company should make more money.

For example, if your goal was to "increase the number of clients we have by 20%", it should be obvious that if you manage to achieve it, you'll increase your revenue.

What's the return on investment?
Whenever you think of a new idea for your site, it's important to think about the *return on investment* (ROI).

If an online shop costs more to build than it brings in through sales, then it's not worth having.

Beware

Many business sites probably make less money over the course of their lifetime than they cost to build.

To make sure yours isn't one of them, it's important to define clear goals and to have an idea of how much money your site could realistically earn.

Defining your brand

Unless you're already a well-known company, somebody visiting your site for the first time probably won't know anything about you. So their first impression of your company will be based *solely* on your website – and everyone knows first impressions count.

The way your website looks and works could make the difference between winning a new customer or losing them for life, so it's vitally important to give a good impression of your company.

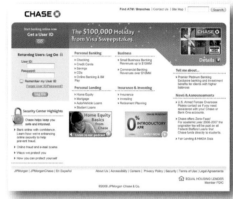

Looks matter, but so does personality

The look-and-feel of your website will affect your visitors' impressions of your company. If your site's bright and funky, your visitors will think you are too. If it's staid and conservative, then so are you, and if it's amateurish and disorganized...

It's important to decide how you want your customers to perceive your company. Try to think of your business as having a personality. Fanta probably want people to think of them as "young, exotic and sexy", while Chase may want people to think of them as "trustworthy and reliable".

Your brand is more than just a logo

You'll often hear people talking in emotional terms about a company. You might "hate" your credit card company or "trust" your bank. This emotional connection to a business is what people call your *brand*, and it takes more than a logo to create one.

If your website looks great but is slow, full of spelling mistakes and prone to crashing, people won't want to do business with you. If you forget to answer emails or process orders, you're going to lose customers no matter how fantastic your logo is.

Hot tip

The more people hear your name, the more they'll remember you.

To strengthen your brand, put your web address on receipts, business cards, emails and answering machine messages – anywhere you can think of in fact.

Standing out from the crowd

When people search for a product or service on the Web, they normally visit several sites before deciding which company to use.

So, it's highly desirable that your website stays in your visitors' memory—and for the right reasons.

It's obviously important that your site is well designed, has good content and loads quickly. However, you also need to ensure it looks different from your competition. Otherwise, why would people choose you, rather than them?

Both Tiffany and Cartier sell high-end jewelry, but their sites each have a distinctive look-and-feel

Dare to be different

It's sometimes tempting to look at your competitors' sites and assume yours should have the same content, along with a similar look-and-feel.

It's certainly useful to look at your competitors' sites. However, ask yourself, "Why would a customer choose my site over my rival?" If your site has similar design and content, then there's no reason for people to pick you instead. In fact, there's a real danger that you'll look like a cheap copy of them.

Your business should have a *unique selling point* (USP), which separates you from your competition. For example, you might be cheaper, quicker or have more variety than anyone else.

Make sure this USP comes across on your website. Your visitor wants to know why they should choose you over anyone else. It's your job to make sure your site answers this question clearly.

Content management

Creating a web page is a skill which requires both creative flair and technical knowledge. It also takes time. Wouldn't it be great if there was a way to add web pages to your site quickly, without having to worry about the design and coding, so you could concentrate on writing good content? Well, there is.

An easy way to edit pages

A *Content management system* (CMS) allows a website owner to add content to their website (as well as edit or delete existing content), without needing to know HTML.

The website owner usually has to log on to a password-protected web page on their server to make changes to the site, although there are some cheaper CMS packages, like Adobe Contribute, which run as applications on your computer.

The very simplest CMS packages might only let you edit words and headings on existing web pages. More complex ones will allow you to add pages or sections and upload images.

Beware

Setting up a CMS is more complicated than creating a web page.

Unless you're an experienced programmer, you may need to pay a professional to set one up for you.

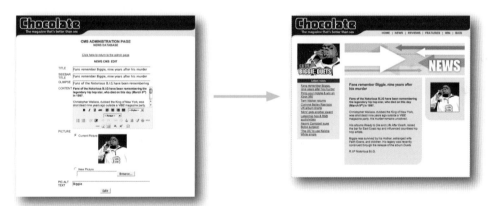

Sharing the workload

One huge advantage of having a CMS is that anyone within your company can update your website. You can make various people within your firm responsible for different sections of the site.

What does a CMS cost?

The simplest CMS packages are free, while the most expensive cost hundreds of thousands of dollars. Expanse (**expansecms.com** – $30) and Adobe Contribute (**adobe.com/contribute** – $150) are both realistic options for small business sites. You can also get a web developer to write a custom CMS for you.

Web databases

A *database* is a collection of information (or data) stored on a computer. Databases are used a lot in business. You might store a list of clients (with addresses, emails and telephone numbers) in a database or perhaps the records of all your stock.

Any information that can be stored in a database, can be stored in an online database, which can be accessed through your website.

For example, a real estate agent might have a database of properties for sale. Traditionally, potential buyers would come to his or her office looking for properties, and the real estate agent would look through the database while the customer waited.

By putting the database online, the customer can search for houses themselves and contact the real estate agent to arrange a viewing when they'd found a suitable property.

How do web databases work?

Databases, like MySQL or Access, only store information (like a name or phone number); they don't know what to do with it.

By contrast, web browsers can only show HTML-based web pages; they can't interpret information from a database. So, to turn the data from a database into a web page you need to process it.

That's where web programming languages like PHP, ASP and Java come in. A typical website might have a PHP program, which takes information from a MySQL database and creates an HTML page, which you can see in your browser.

Hot tip

For more information about web databases, turn to page 17.

Ecommerce

These days, having a website is very common among businesses. However, many corporate websites are purely for marketing. You can find out about the company, get phone numbers, prices and even fill in an inquiry form. Marketing sites like these, with pages like "about us" and "contact us", are often called *brochureware* sites because they're basically just online brochures.

Some companies have sites where you can actually carry out business. The most well-known examples of *ecommerce* sites are online shops, like Amazon and the auction site eBay. However, any site that lets you carry out all or part of your business with a company is an ecommerce site.

Before ecommerce websites, investing could only be done by visiting your financial advisor or calling your broker.

Now you can buy shares and invest in funds instantly online.

What kind of ecommerce sites are there?

Almost any part of your business can be done online, as long as it doesn't involve physically moving or manipulating objects.

For example, a printer might allow advertising agencies and graphic designers to log on to their website, place an order for some brochures or posters, upload PDFs of the design and then pay for it. All that's left to do is print the order and deliver it.

Online shops

Online shops are big business. Web-only retailers, like Amazon, compete with traditional retailers' online shops, like Barnes & Noble (**bn.com**), for a share of a massive market.

Beware

If you've got a large and complex inventory of products, it's easy to spend a fortune developing a complex online shop to sell them.

Starting with a smaller shop that sells a few of your simpler products online, will let you test the market. You can use any profit made from the site to develop it further.

Online shops can be set up cheaply and easily with a shopping cart system like Shopify (**shopify.com**).

Online shops vs. shopping carts

The terms "shopping cart" and "online shop" often get used interchangeably–but there's a difference. An *online shop* is a site (or part of a site) that allows visitors to buy things over the Web. A *shopping cart* is a way for an online shop to keep track of what you've decided to buy, as you move through the site.

If you've got a really small online shop that only sells a few products, you might not need a shopping cart, as you can fit them all on one page.

However, most shops will use a shopping cart, as well as a product database, search and an online credit card processing system.

How much do online shops cost?

It's possible to set up an online shop for just a few dollars (and with no programming knowledge), using a hosted shopping cart like Shopify (**shopify.com**) or Big Cartel (**bigcartel.com**). They're a good option for small businesses, but you normally won't have much control over the way the shop works.

Larger retailers are likely to use a high-end online shop, or to pay a web developer or web design company to create a custom-built ecommerce site, which meets their needs exactly.

Selling online with eBay

eBay has over 150 million users worldwide and nearly 80 million in the US alone. That's a lot of potential customers spending a lot of money. If your business sells any kind of product, the likelihood is someone on eBay will want one.

How does eBay work?

There are two main ways to sell things on eBay: auctions and fixed price sales.

eBay auctions are similar to ordinary auctions – you set a starting price, you can name a reserve and then people bid on your item. At the end of the auction, the person who bid the most wins.

Fixed price sales, or as eBay calls them "Buy it now" sales, are just like ordinary sales in a shop. You fix a price and if your customers are happy to buy at that price, then they will.

Hot tip

Even if you've got your own online shop, selling your products on eBay can provide a valuable extra source of revenue for your business.

Taking payment

One advantage of using eBay is that they have their own credit card processing system, called PayPal, which you can use to take payments for products you've sold. You can also arrange with the buyer to be paid by check, wired funds or bank transfer.

How do I get started?

Becoming an eBay seller is very straightforward. Signing up takes minutes, though you'll need to provide all your personal and business information, as well as some financial information, like credit card or bank details, so eBay can check your identity. Once you've signed up, you can start selling straight away.

Hot tip

For more information on becoming an eBay seller (or buyer), see the eBay title in this series.

Getting paid

If you're doing business online, the chances are you want to take payment online too. Online credit card processing has been around for over a decade and is now very easy to set up.

The options

If you want to take payment online, you've got several options:

PayPal

The first and easiest option is PayPal. PayPal accounts are easy to set up and you can take credit card payments straight away.

PayPal takes a percentage (2-3%) of each transaction, and the rest of the money goes into your PayPal account. You can then transfer this money into your bank account. PayPal is very well known, so people are likely to trust it to be safe.

Internet merchant account

Alternatively, you could set up an *internet merchant account* with your bank, and use an online credit card processing firm like **worldpay.com** or **verisign.com**, to handle the credit card transactions.

Depending on the provider, the money may be transferred into your bank account straight away or several weeks after the transaction.

You'll have to pay a set up fee and a fixed monthly fee, as well as a charge per transaction, so this is an option for people who expect to sell reasonably large volumes on their website.

Security

So that your customer's credit card details are safe, you need to ensure they're sent over the Internet securely.

This is done by encrypting the credit card details and sending them over a secure (or *https*) connection. You can tell if you're using a secure connection, as your browser will display a padlock icon ( ) in the browser's *address bar* (where you type in URLs).

Luckily, if you're using an online credit card processor, like Worldpay or PayPal, they'll almost certainly handle all of the online security for you.

Hot tip

There are alternatives to PayPal, like **propay.com** or **nochex.com**, which allow you to take credit cards, without needing to set up an internet merchant account.

Beware

If you already have credit card processing facilities, you might be tempted to ask customers to email their credit card details to you, either directly or using a web form. Don't! A criminal could easily intercept an email.

(13) Personal sites and blogs

It's never been easier to set up your own site or blog.

Why create your own site?

Creating a personal website can be hugely rewarding. They're a great way to share your opinions, knowledge and experience with others, whether it's in-depth knowledge of your home town or a lifetime's experience as a boat builder.

They're also a great way for your friends and family to keep up to date with what's going on in your life, especially if you're going through an interesting experience, like traveling through Asia or bringing up your first child.

It's easy

There are two main ways to create your own site. First, you could rent some space on a web server and create a site (either using hand-coded HTML or a visual web design program like Dreamweaver).

Alternatively, you could set up a blog using a website like **blogger.com** or **wordpress.com**

The advantage of blogs is that they're very easy to set up and add to, so you can spend more time concentrating on the content and less worrying about the design or the HTML.

Web designer Paul Boag has a popular blog and podcast* about web design. As well as providing a useful resource for aspiring web designers, the site has increased his company's profile.

148

It's great PR

If you're in business, you might think it would be a waste of time creating a personal site. However, a well written blog can be a great way to increase your company's profile and drive traffic to your main website.

If you're an experienced plumber, for instance, why not share your knowledge with other people? A site teaching people the basics of plumbing will gain you a reputation as an expert, people may link to your articles and someone might even give you a call, next time they need a pipe fixed.

*Podcasts (or "iPod broadcasts") are radio style shows that your computer downloads automatically whenever a new show is published.

Set up a blog with Blogger

Blogs are a bit like online diaries. They're small, easy to update sites created by one person about something that interests them. There are blogs on everything from web design to the war in Iraq.

Creating a blog is incredibly simple, especially with Blogger, Google's blog service. In just three steps you can set one up.

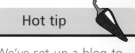

Hot tip

We've set up a blog to accompany this book. See page 182 for details.

Blogs are a great way to tell people about things the mainstream media doesn't cover.

A documentary about a controversial dam in India, is unlikely to get much coverage in major newspapers or TV, but you can add a blog entry about it yourself.

1 Create an account

Before you can do anything you'll need to set up a Blogger account. Choose a username and password, fill in your email address and you're good to go.

2 Name your blog

The next step is to decide on a title for your blog and a web address, so other people can find it. As well as searching through Google, people can reach your blog by typing the web address into their browser, for example, **myblog.blogspot.com**

3 Choose your template

Blogger gives you dozens of templates to choose from, so you can control how your blog will look.

That's it! Once you've set up your blog, you can log in and start posting articles.

Create an online resumé

One area that's really taken off since the Web started is online recruitment. There are literally thousands of job sites covering every conceivable type of vacancy, from construction workers to computer engineers. In fact, many people now search for work *exclusively* though websites.

A web page containing your resumé is very useful if you're looking for work through websites. Rather than emailing your resumé to hundreds of potential employers, you can just send them a link.

The best online resumés are much more than HTML versions of a Word document.

New York photographer, Peter Hurley, uses his site to showcase his work in a clean, creative way.

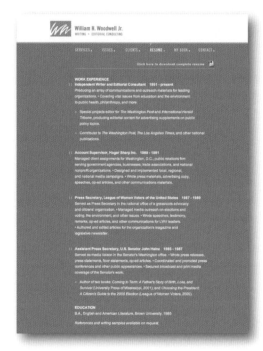

Thanks to **peterhurley.com**, **illgraphs.com** and William H. Woodwell, Jr.

How do I create an online resumé?

The easiest way to create an online resumé is to use a recruitment site like **monster.com**, which lets you add your details using a web form. You'll be able to send prospective employers a link to your resumé, or employers can search the site for suitable candidates.

If you'd rather have a more tailored resumé, you can create a web page yourself, using HTML or some web design software like Dreamweaver. You can make the page's design as simple or as creative as you like, but make sure the employer can print it.

14 Reaching the widest audience

A website can reach millions of people relatively easily and cheaply. However, with a little extra thought and effort, you can reach even more.

Testing on different browsers

Which browser do you use to look at the Web? For most people the answer is Internet Explorer.

But IE, as it's known, isn't the only browser available. Apple Mac users, for instance, usually use a browser called Safari. After Internet Explorer, the most popular browser for Windows PCs is Firefox, which is used by over 200 million people worldwide. Other well-known browsers include Netscape (once the world's leading browser), Opera and Mozilla.

Worse news still for web designers is the fact that the browser manufacturers have released various different versions of each of these browsers over the years, as they try to improve their software and outdo their competitors. The latest version of Internet Explorer is IE7.

The old **gap.com** site looked great in Internet Explorer, but couldn't be seen at all using Safari on an Apple Mac.

As Macs are expensive, Safari users tend to have a high income, so Gap would have missed out on some very valuable customers.

Luckily, the problem's now been fixed.

So why should I care about all these browsers?

Because they're different programs, each browser renders web pages differently and each has its own bugs. A site that looks perfect in Internet Explorer 6 or 7, might look totally different in Internet Explorer 5 or Firefox. In fact, it might not work at all.

Before you launch your website, it's important to test it in all the main browsers, especially if you plan to make any money from it. All the browsers we've mentioned are free to download, so it won't cost you anything to test your site on them. Not testing your site, on the other hand, could cost you customers or sales.

What do I do if I find a problem?

Fix it, basically. You might find that the problem is a small cosmetic one. For instance, there could be more space between the headline and the text than you wanted – in which case you might be able to ignore it.

However, sometimes you'll find the site looks completely broken in one or more browsers, so you'll need to find out what's causing the problem.

Sites like **quirksmode.org** have information about the bugs each of the common browsers has.

You'll probably find you get fewer problems (and ones that are easier to fix) if you've used a web standards approach from the start, when building your site.

Web standards

If you want your site to be used by as many people as possible, then you should build it using *web standards*.

What are web standards?
"Web standards" are, basically, an approach to building websites that ensure they work correctly in any modern browser.

Web standards sites use a combination of technologies, namely XHTML, CSS and unobtrusive Javascript (also called DOM scripting).

What's the big deal?
If you've just started learning web design, you're lucky–you can use web standards to build a site that works in different browsers without too much effort–but things weren't always this easy.

Most web designers want to be able to create attractive websites with magazine-quality photography and print-like layouts. However, the Web was designed to share scientific information, not to be a marketing tool. As a result, HTML is great for marking up physics papers, but very poorly designed for producing attractive, commercial websites.

To get round the limitations of HTML, web designers used to use HTML tags in ways they were not designed for. For example, using data tables to position elements on the page (see page 130). As well as being inefficient, this approach caused problems getting sites to look right on different browsers.

At one time, this old-fashioned approach was the only reliable way of producing attractive websites. However, for the last few years, the main browsers have supported CSS fairly well, making a modern, web standards approach to building websites possible.

So what are the advantages of web standards?
Web standards sites are better than other sites for several reasons:

- They should work perfectly on any modern browser
- They are quicker to load
- They tend to appear higher on search engines
- They're accessible to people with disabilities
- They'll work on older browsers, even if they don't look perfect
- They can work on other devices like PDAs or Web TV
- You can change the design of your site easily

Hot tip

For more information about web standards, visit **webstandards.org** or pick up a copy of **XHTML in easy steps** and **CSS in easy steps**.

153

Beware

Many people still do things the old-fashioned, non-standards way– mainly because they haven't had the time to learn modern web standards techniques.

If you're learning HTML and CSS, make sure you use books and websites that teach you web standards, not old-fashioned, table-based web development.

Does your site speak Chinese?

There are hundreds of millions of people using the Web and it's easy to forget that not all of them speak English. In fact, only around a quarter of Internet users are native English speakers.

After English, the most spoken language online is Chinese, followed by Japanese, Spanish, German and French.

Does this affect me?

If you run a small firm, you might not think you need to worry about people half-way around the world—but don't be so sure. If you were planning a vacation to Beijing, would you look at hotels with sites in English or Chinese? Well, a Chinese person coming to your city will most likely choose a hotel with a site in Chinese, if one exists.

Similarly, a Mexican looking for an iPod would be more likely to buy one if the site was in Spanish.

How can I translate my site?

If you've coded your site well (ideally using web standards), Google can translate your site automatically from English to several common languages including French, Spanish and Chinese. Just don't expect the translation to be very good.

A better alternative is to hire a translator. This is obviously a more expensive option, but ask yourself how much you'd be prepared to pay to reach millions of extra customers.

There are over 100 million Chinese-speaking web users, more than any language except English.

Introducing accessibility

Millions of people around the world have disabilities that make it hard to use badly produced websites. People who are blind, for instance, often use special software called a *screen reader* to listen to a web page. They sometimes find it impossible to use image-heavy websites, unless a text-only alternative is provided for them.

People who are color blind may find certain combinations of colors hard to read, such as green text on a red background, while anyone whose disability prevents them from using a mouse might find it hard to navigate a site with DHTML drop-down menus.

In most countries, including America, Britain and Australia, there are now laws making it illegal to discriminate against disabled people – and that includes producing websites they can't access.

Accessibility is the practice of making websites as easy to use as possible for people with disabilities.

How can a blind person see a website?
They can't. But they can read it, using a braille ticker tape, or hear it, using special screen reader software.

Accessibility is mostly technical
A lot of people think accessible websites need to look ugly. In fact, nothing could be further from the truth. Most of the things that make a site accessible (or not) are to do with the way the HTML is coded. There are some minor limitations on the design, but these will often make your site better for all of your visitors.

Disabled people are potential customers
There are around 10 million blind or partially-sighted people in the USA alone. That's a lot of potential customers. Stopping them from using your website isn't just rude – it's bad business.

Google – the blind billionaire
Imagine if you knew a blind billionaire with millions of friends, who spent her whole life visiting websites and telling all her friends about the sites she liked. Would you want her to be able to visit your site? Of course you would.

Well, if you were asked to describe Google, you could do a lot worse than, "a blind billionaire with millions of friends". Because Google is a computer program, it can't see images. So, if your site is image-heavy, it won't get a good ranking – unless it's accessible.

155

Don't forget

Accessibility isn't just about making sites that blind people can use, although that is important.

Deaf people, dyslexics and people with learning difficulties, all find some sites hard to use. While people who can't use a mouse, because of a physical disability, might not be able to navigate others.

Hot tip

Accessibility makes good business sense.

When Legal and General, a British financial services company, made their site accessible, they got 30% more search engine traffic, saved $350k a year on site maintenance and increased online life insurance sales by 90%.

Top 7 accessibility tips

Accessibility can be a fairly complicated subject. Ideally, you'll use web standards, but there are some simple things you can do to dramatically improve the accessibility of any site.

1 **Write meaningful ALT text**

ALT text is read aloud to blind users who can't see an image, by their screen reader. Without ALT text your site might be virtually unusable for a blind visitor, so make sure you add it to all your images (see page 90 for more info).

2 **Use a spell checker**

Screen readers don't know how to pronounce misspelled words. Their "guesses" can confuse blind people, so try to make as few mistakes as possible.

3 **Avoid abbrevs. if you can**

Without help, screen readers can't tell an abbreviation isn't a word, so they'll often try to pronounce it. You might read the letters "nr" as "near", but a screen reader may guess at "ner". Either use the full word or add an `<abbr>` tag (with the full word or phrase in a `title` attribute).

4 **Use high contrast colors, especially for text**

Dark text on a light or white background is best for most people as it increases readability.

5 **Make text scalable**

Partially-sighted people and other people with poor eyesight need to be able to resize text. Internet Explorer doesn't let you resize text that's been set using pixels (px), so use points (pt) or ems (em) for text sizes instead.

6 **Use CSS to set colors**

Then, if your visitor finds your default stylesheet hard to use, they can turn it off or use their own default stylesheet.

7 **Ensure links make sense out of context**

Blind people often skip through the links on a page, so it's important your links make sense out of context. "Click here" doesn't mean anything on its own, so say, "Click here for more information about cell phones," instead.

Designing for multiple devices

When most people think of the Web, they imagine someone sitting in front of a PC using Internet Explorer. However, PCs aren't the only way to look at a website.

PDAs, cell phones and even some TVs can be used to access web pages – if the site has been designed to work on them.

How do I get my site to work on a PDA?

If you've used a web standards approach to build your website, it will be fairly easy to get the site to work on other devices. All you need to do is build a new stylesheet so the device knows how to display your pages.

If your site uses old-fashioned techniques, like tables, you may have to build a separate site for people who use PDAs.

What's the difference?

Compared to a PC, a PDA has a very small screen. While a typical PC might have an 800 x 600 pixel screen (or higher), PDAs can have screens that are as small as 160 x 160 pixels.

Also, PC screens are generally landscape (i.e. they're wider than they are tall) whereas PDAs are often portrait.

If you're designing a site for a PDA or a cell phone, you'll need to cut out a lot of the elements you have on your standard website. Anything that's not 100% relevant to the page needs to go; there's certainly no room for large decorative images or extended copyright messages.

Hot tip

CSS allows you to attach several stylesheets to a page for use by different devices, using the media attribute. For example media="tv" or media="handheld".

For more information, see **CSS in easy steps**.

157

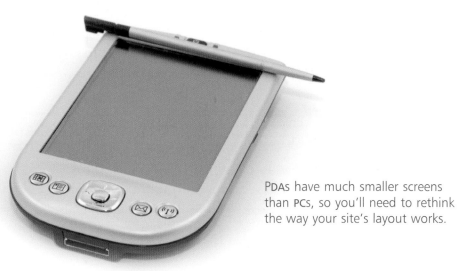

PDAs have much smaller screens than PCs, so you'll need to rethink the way your site's layout works.

Frames & why not to use them

Frames are a way to show more than one web page in your browser window at the same time. The main reason people use frames is so they can keep part of their design, like the navigation, in one place while the rest of the design scrolls.

This sounds useful and it is. Unfortunately, frames have lots of drawbacks which generally outweigh any advantages.

The problem(s) with frames

Although there are some limited uses for frames, it's generally not a good idea to use them. There are entire websites dedicated to all the problems with frames, but here are just a few of the reasons frames are bad:

- Your site will do worse in search engines
- Your visitors won't be able to print your pages properly
- Disabled people will find your site much harder to use
- You'll have to write different code for different browsers
- Your visitors won't be able to bookmark pages in your site
- People who reach your site through a search engine won't see your navigation

There are fixes for some of these problems, but it's much better to avoid them altogether.

There is another way

Perhaps the best reason to avoid frames is that you can create exactly the same effect within one page using css, by using the `overflow: auto;` property. It's outside the scope of this book to explain the technique in full, but it's very simple to do.

Hot tip

For more information about css scrolling areas, read **css in easy steps**.

158

15 Launching your site

So, you've finally finished your site. All the content's written, the design's done and the HTML coded. Now what?

Choosing a web host

People around the world use the Web at all hours of the day and night. So, if they're going to be able to see your website, you'll need to host it on a suitable computer that's permanently connected to the Internet, known as a *server*.

You could set up a server in your bedroom, but it's cheaper, easier and more reliable to get a *web hosting company* to host your site on a professional server.

Prices start from a few dollars a year, going up to several thousand dollars a month for top of the line web hosting. The more visitors your site gets, the more you'll need to pay.

As well as your website, most hosting companies will host your email accounts as well, allowing you to set up your own personalized email addresses (*me@mycompany.com*).

Many will also allow you to run programming languages like PHP or ASP and set up a database.

Decide what you need before you choose a host

Before you choose a web host, it's important to decide what features you'll need from your *web hosting account*. For example, will you need a server-side programming language like PHP or a database like MYSQL? What about web statistics (see page 180)?

If your site is likely to be busy, you may need a *high-bandwidth* hosting account, otherwise you could face extra charges, or even have your account suspended, when your site gets lots of visitors.

Most hosting companies give you a password protected *control panel* you can log into to check your statistics and set up emails.

Find out what level of support your hosting company offers. Will you be able to phone them if you have a problem? Is it a premium rate number? What hours do the support team work?

Hot tip

To find out if other people have had bad experiences with a certain hosting company, search Google for "[Hosting Company] sucks" or "bad experience with [Hosting Company]".

Registering a domain name

Your domain name is like a phone number for the Web. It's a unique name given to your site and ends in a short extension like **.com**, **.net** or **.co.uk**

How do I choose a domain name?

Domain names are a lot like phone numbers – and, like phone numbers, it helps if they are memorable. Lots of names have been taken already, but it's always possible to come up with something people can easily remember.

Make sure your name's easy to spell and can't be confused with any other words – **beachfurniture.com** could easily be mixed up with **beechfurniture.com**

If you choose a domain name with keywords in it, this should help improve your search engine ranking for those keywords, as people will be likely to link to you using them. For example, you might link to **scubabvi.com** with the words "scuba BVI".

Which extension should I have?

Normally you should choose a **.com** extension if you can get it, if not try a **.net**

If you're from outside the USA, you should also consider your local extension like **.ca** (Canada), **.co.uk** (Britain) or **.com.au** (Australia). Certain organizations can apply for special extensions like **.edu** (education) or **.org** (non-profit groups like charities).

How do I register one and what's the cost?

Most web hosts allow you to register domain names when you set up your web hosting, or you could try a site like **godaddy.com** or **123-reg.co.uk**

It's often easiest to register your domain name with the same firm that hosts your site, because there's less configuration involved.

Prices vary quite a lot, so it might be worth shopping around. You should be able to register a **.com** domain name for under $10 a year and some country-specific domains (like **.co.uk**) are even cheaper.

If you decide to use a professional web designer, they should be able to register your domain for you.

Uploading your site

So, after weeks of hard work, you've finally finished your website and now you want to put it online. But how do you do that? Well, it's actually quite easy.

Putting your site on your server

By now, you should have arranged a server to host your site (if you haven't, see 160). So that people can see your site on the Web, you'll need to transfer it to your server, using some special software called an FTP (or file transfer protocol) program.

FTP programs are usually cheap and there are even free ones available, like Coffee Cup Free FTP (**www.coffeecup.com/free-ftp**). Many web design programs, like Dreamweaver, also have built-in FTP software.

Hot tip

Some web design programs, like Dreamweaver, have built-in FTP, so you can upload files to your server with the touch of a button.

To connect to your web server, you'll need to know:

- The address of your FTP server. For example, **ftp.mysite.com**
- The username of your account
- Your FTP password

Once you've connected to your web server, you should be able to *upload* files to it or *download* them to your computer. Exactly how you do this will depend on the FTP program you're using, but often you can simply drag-and-drop files and folders.

Once you've uploaded files to your web server, you should be able to see them on the Web, by typing your domain name into your web browser. Provided you had uploaded the files to your server correctly, your website should now appear online for all to see.

Setting up email accounts

Once you own your domain name, you can set up custom email addresses, like *peter.piper@yoursite.com*

Your hosting account should have a web-based *control panel* that allows you to log on and make changes to your account, including adding and editing email addresses.

Once you've set up an email address, there are several ways to handle emails sent to it.

Forwarding
The simplest way to handle emails is to *forward* them to another email address. For example, you could forward all emails sent to *info@yoursite.com* to your Hotmail or Gmail account.

Mailboxes
Most people have a *mailbox* where all their email goes. This is basically a folder on your email server that stores all your emails. You can then download them using an email program, like Outlook Express, or look at them online using a *webmail account*.

When you set up an email, you need to choose a username and password. Then, you need to configure your email program to download emails from your mailbox. As well as your username and password, you have to tell the program where the email is stored. This is called an *incoming mail server* (or POP *server*).

Default routing
If somebody tries to send an email to an email address you haven't set up, you can do one of two things with it. First, you could "bounce" the email back to the sender. Alternatively, you could forward it to another email address. Your control panel should allow you to set up *default routing*, so that any unrecognized emails would go to one predefined address, like *info@mysite.com*

Outgoing email
As well as setting up your email program, like Outlook Express, to receive emails, you'll need to set it up to send them.

Usually, all you need to do is tell it which *outgoing mail server* (or SMTP *server*) to send the email to. Unlike the incoming mail server, the outgoing mail server is usually supplied by your Internet Service Provider (ISP). For example, your outgoing mail server might be **smtp.charter.net** if your ISP is Charter.

Beware

If AOL is your ISP, then you may have trouble sending emails through Outlook Express.

AOL doesn't properly support the SMTP protocol for sending emails.

Testing your site

Once you've uploaded your site to the server, it's important to test it on as many computers and web browsers as possible, in order to check everything's working as you expect.

You should have done regular testing while you were building your site, to ensure it worked in the major web browsers. This is your chance to make sure there are no remaining problems.

Test your links
You also need to check that all the links on your site work. If your site is small, you could do this manually, or you could use a program which will automatically check them all like REL Link Checker for Windows (**www.relsoftware.com/rlc/**) or Link Checker for Mac (**www.dotsw.com/linkchecker.html**).

Check your spelling
While you're testing your site, you should get somebody to check every page for spelling mistakes and other errors in the text, that may have crept in while you were building it.

Test your forms
Before you launch your site, you need to test all of your forms to check they're working as expected.

Make sure you don't *only* type valid information into the form fields. People who visit your site will make mistakes and your forms need to be able to deal with them. Try putting an email address into the phone number field and see what happens.

Hopefully, everything will work perfectly. However, if it doesn't, now is your last chance to correct any mistakes, before the public sees your site.

What is (and isn't) pre-launch testing
It's important you don't get confused about what you're testing for.

If you're just about to launch your site, it isn't the right time to look at the design and say, "Do you think we should have made the background blue?"

It's also not the time to get users to test your site. You should have done that very early on in the design process, before you went ahead and built the whole site. Pre-launch testing is only done to spot bugs and mistakes.

16 Promoting your site

It takes a lot to create a successful website. A well thought out sitemap, creative design and snappy writing are all important if you want your site to succeed. However, if your site doesn't get any visitors, all that work was a bit pointless, wasn't it? Promotion is often overlooked, but it's often as important to a successful website as all the other aspects put together.

Location, location, location

In the real world, the secret to a successful shop or restaurant is the location. Sure, good products, a well-designed building and attentive staff are all important—but if you don't get paying customers through the door, you won't make any money.

The same is true on the Web. The single most important thing with any website is to get people to visit it. Without visitors, a stunning design, well-coded HTML and sharply written content are just a waste of time and effort.

So, how can you get people to visit your website?

Well, if you're eBay or Microsoft you can run ads on TV, radio and in glossy magazines. Of course, most people don't have anywhere near the kind of budget to do this—but don't panic, there are many other ways to get people to visit your site that won't break the bank.

The most well-known way to get people coming to your site is through a search engine, like Google. Think about it, that's how you find most of the sites you visit, isn't it?

It's not that hard to get listed on Google and its competitors, but that doesn't guarantee people will visit your site. Remember, you're competing with over 25 billion other web pages.

If you're lucky, your site will naturally perform well in Google for some *keywords* (see page 169), but usually it won't. Helping your site perform as well as possible in search engines is called *search engine optimization* (or SEO).

Alternatives to SEO

Search engine optimization gets a lot of attention, but there are plenty of other ways to attract people to your site.

For example, you can pay to advertise through a *pay-per-click* scheme like Google AdWords. You pay a set fee every time somebody clicks on an ad for your site.

Other alternatives include blogging, podcasting, sending out a press release and traditional advertising through local newspapers or flyers.

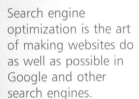

Don't forget

Search engine optimization is the art of making websites do as well as possible in Google and other search engines.

Search engine optimization

Unless you've got a huge advertising budget, your site's success will likely depend on how many people find it via search engines.

Google is currently the biggest search engine by far, with around 50% of all searches going through it. Yahoo comes next (about 25%) followed by MSN (10%), AOL (6%) and Ask (3%).

Getting your site onto the major search engines is obviously important, but, with over 25 billion web pages currently indexed by Google, how can you ensure people will find *your* site?

Helping your site perform well in search engines

Search engine optimization, or SEO for short, is the art of making web pages perform as well as possible in Google and the other major search engines.

There are hundreds of techniques to help web pages appear higher up the search engines' results page. However, most can be split into two types of technique: on-site and off-site optimization.

On-site optimization is any technique that involves changing the actual website (like changing page titles or adding extra pages), while off-site optimization involves doing things which don't change the website (like getting other sites to link to yours).

To do well, you'll need to use both on-site and off-site techniques in your SEO strategy.

Time doesn't stand still – nor does SEO

Search engines are among the biggest companies in the world. Their business depends on you, their customer, being able to find relevant web pages when you search for something.

Unscrupulous business owners are constantly trying to trick search engines into giving them artificially high positions. That's good news for them, but bad for Google's users. If you've searched for "Florida modeling agency", you're unlikely to want diet pills.

Because of this, search engines are constantly having to change the formula, or *algorithm*, they use to rank web pages.

If you read a book on SEO from the 1990s, most of the techniques it describes will be obsolete. So, it's important to keep up to date by reading SEO websites and blogs. Even the techniques described in this book will eventually become obsolete.

Hot tip

There are lots of great resources on the Web about SEO, some of the best include:

- **searchenginewatch.com**
- **seobook.com**
- **seomoz.org**
- **seroundtable.com**
- **mr-seo.com**

Beware

Because search engines don't want to be spammed, they keep the way they rank web pages (their *algorithm*) top secret.

Although SEO experts can work out roughly how Google ranks web pages, nobody can be 100% sure and even the experts often disagree.

Submitting your site to Google

If you want people to visit your site, you need to be listed on Google. Google has a computer program, called a *spider*, that automatically goes through the Web and adds every web page to its database. However, it can't look at your site unless it knows it exists. So here's how you tell Google about your site.

1 **Click on the 'About Google' link**

The first thing you need to do is go to Google's homepage. At the bottom of the page you'll see a link that says "**About Google.**" Click on it.

2 **Click on 'Submit your content to Google'**

On the next page, you'll see a link that says "**Submit your content to Google.**" Click on it.

3 **Click on 'Add your URL to Google's Index'**

On the following page, you'll see a link that says "**Add your URL to Google's index.**" Click on it.

4 **Type in your web address**

The final stage of the process is to type in the main web address (or URL) of your site. Google can take anywhere between a few days and a few months, to add your site to its index.

Keywords: what they are and how to use them

Keywords are words or phrases that people search for on Google*.

*Or any other search engine.

For example, if you search Google for "easy steps books", the keywords you are looking for are "easy", "steps" and "books". Any page that contains all three of those words will come up in the search results (around 50 million do at the moment).

The first step towards performing well in Google is to compile a list of keywords and phrases you want your site to rank well for.

What do you do with your keywords?

Once you've made your list of keywords (really you should be looking at *key phrases*; individual words are usually too competitive), you should create at least one page on your site which is optimized for each of them.

For example, if you're doing a site for a Thai food restaurant in New York, you might have the following key phrases:

- Thai food restaurant
- Thai food New York
- New York restaurant

Then, for each of those key phrases you create a page that's *optimized* for them, which means you include the key phrase:

- in the URL, with each keyword separated by a hyphen (-). For example, **www.mysite.com/thai-food-new-york.html**
- in the `<title>` tag
- in the main heading (the `<h1>` tag) and, if possible, some of the sub-headings (`<h2>`, `<h3>`)
- several times in the first 200-300 words of content
- in the ALT text of some of the images
- in the text for inbound links to that page. This includes links from other pages on your site, as well as links from other sites to yours (where you have control over this)

Also, if you use your main keywords in your domain name, ideally separated by hyphens, it can help your position in Google for them. For example, **web-design-book.com** or **mr-seo.com**

Hot tip

Not all keywords are equal. More people will search for "hotels" than "hotels in Kentucky".

However, it's also harder to rank well for "hotels" than "hotels in Kentucky".

So, it's a good idea to select a range of keywords to optimize for.

Choose one competitive keyword that gets lots of traffic, as well as a few longer key phrases that are less competitive, but get less traffic.

Goodkeywords.com is a free program for Windows that helps you choose keywords.

Inside the mind of Google

When you search for something in Google, you are given a list of web pages that contain the keywords you were looking for.

For example, if you searched for "Seattle hotels", you'd be given a list of web pages that contain the words "Seattle" and "hotels".

For many keywords, there are several million web pages which match the search. So, which ones does Google show you first? Well, Google ranks web pages based on a number of factors.

Keyword position and density

First, it looks at where the keywords appear in the page and how often they appear. A page that uses the words "hotel" and "Seattle" several times in the first few paragraphs, is much more likely to be about hotels in Seattle, than one where the words appear once in passing, at the bottom of the page.

Important tags

Google gives more weight to text that appears in certain HTML tags, like the `<title>` tag, headings (`<h1>`) and sub-headings (`<h2>` or `<h3>`). It considers text in these tags to be more important than ordinary text on the page.

For example, a page that has the words "Scuba diving in Egypt" in the `<title>` tag is highly likely to be about Egyptian scuba diving. Likewise, it's a reasonable bet that a page with "Novelty chess boards" as one of the main headings (`<h1>` or `<h2>`) will be about novelty chess boards.

Link popularity

Another important factor Google uses to determine how high your page appears in a search, is to look at the other pages that link to it. Google counts each link to your web page as a "vote" for that page. The idea is that if lots of people link to your site, they probably think it's a good one.

Page rank

Google assigns each page on the Internet a number between 0 and 10, called its *page rank* or PR. A page with a page rank of 10 (PR10) is very popular and will generally be listed higher in search results than an unpopular page, like one with PR0. All other things being equal, sites with a high PR generally appear higher in Google than ones that don't.

Beware

Google can usually tell if you're trying to trick it into getting an artificially high ranking.

Using your key phrase once or twice in the first paragraph of your page will help your ranking, but repeating the keyword 500 times is obviously spam and could get you banned from Google altogether.

Hot tip

For more information about doing well on Google, why not read **Getting Noticed on Google in easy steps?**

Link quality

A link from a site with a high page rank will help boost your site's own PR much more than one from a site with a low PR. This is because Google assumes a site with a high PR is already trusted by lots of people, so is likely to link to higher quality sites. So, a link from a popular site, like **cnn.com** or **bbc.co.uk**, is worth far more than a link from **your-small-town-hardware-store.com**

Link text

As well as the number of pages that link to yours, Google also looks at the words they use in the link. If other sites link to yours with the words "hotel database for Seattle", it will improve your ranking for the keywords "hotel database Seattle", but is less likely to do well for "pizza restaurant Miami".

This is another reason why you shouldn't use "click here" as link text. Google will assume the page it links to is about something called "click here", rather than a hotel database for Seattle.

Friendly URLs

Google also looks at the words used in a page's web address (or URL). **Ineasysteps.com/resources/articles/** is more likely to contain some "articles" than **ineasysteps.com/feedback/**

Sites that use server-side programming, like PHP, often have long, ugly URLs that are hard to read and don't contain any keywords, like **mysite.com/index.php?action=user&id=da45b402-1875**

URLs like this harm your chances of doing well in Google, so if possible try not to use them.

You can usually set up your server to use friendly URLs, like the ones on the **ineasysteps.com** site. The most common way to do this is with a technique called *mod_rewrite*. For more information, search Google for "friendly URLs" or "mod_rewrite".

Changes over time

Google examines how your site changes over time, as well as how the sites that link to you change over time.

If you have a small site with only a dozen inbound links, then it would look suspicious if it suddenly got 5,000 links in a few days. It's important to add pages and links gradually, otherwise you could get penalized for spamming Google.

Hot tip

Google is constantly changing the way it ranks sites, in order to keep one step ahead of the cheats.

However, at the moment the *link text* people use when they link to your site is very important in determining which keywords your site will do well for.

If you search Google for "miserable failure", the top result is currently the homepage of American President, George W. Bush, with film-maker Michael Moore a close second.

Neither page includes the phrase; however, thousands of politically-minded bloggers and site owners have linked to these pages using the phrase "miserable failure", forcing them to the top of Google.

3 search engine myths

META tags help you rank well

META tags are tags near the top of your page which aren't shown but carry extra information about it. They look like this:

```
<meta name="keywords" content="web, design, book">
```

Out of date books and websites often claim you should place keywords in your META tags to boost your search engine ranking.

META tags used to be important for the major search engines, but this is no longer true. In fact, using them can actually do more harm to your site than good, unless you're an expert.

Page rank is everything

A page rank is a number between 0 and 10 which Google gives to every page it indexes, based on the number and quality of other web pages that link to it.

Page rank is important, but it's only one factor in determining which pages rank well for any given keyword.

Type "Amandas Glass Art" into Google. The page that currently comes top is the homepage of **www.amandasglassart.co.uk**, which has a page rank of 0. If PR was the only thing that mattered, you would have expected pages like the **bbc.co.uk** or **ebay.com** homepage (both of which have PR 9) to come top, wouldn't you?

An SEO expert can guarantee a number 1 spot

Anybody that promises you they can get you a number one spot is a) a liar, b) a cheat or c) delusional.

An experienced SEO professional will be able to improve your rankings, but can't guarantee a genuine top spot (or even that your site will appear on the first page).

If anybody promises you they can deliver a top ten spot or number one position, you should avoid them like the plague.

They may try to get you ranked for a long or obscure key phrase nobody would ever search for, like "web designer in Cornwall that used to live in the BVI".

Even worse, they may promise to get you the top listing for your own company name. How many other companies called "Barnes & Noble" are there?

Don't forget

SEO isn't an exact science. There's lots of out of date and incorrect information on the Web, so it's important to find sources of information you can trust.

Just because you read something on a blog you stumbled across, doesn't make it true.

Why web standards matter

Sites which are accessible to blind visitors and use web standards techniques (like XHTML and CSS), tend to do better in Google than other sites. This might sound strange, but there are several good reasons for this being true.

Web standards pages have less code in them. Search engines judge how important your keywords are by where they appear on the page. A page that contains the word "tennis" right at the top is more likely to be about tennis than one that mentions the word, in passing, at the bottom of the page.

Old-fashioned, table-based pages often have dozens, or even hundreds, of lines of HTML code or Javascript before the first word of actual content. A search engine doesn't realize this code isn't content and will treat the first sentence as if it appears half-way down the page.

Similarly, search engines treat headings (`<h1>`, `<h2>` tags) as more important than ordinary text. A page that has "Nike sneakers" as the main title is highly likely to be about Nike sneakers. Since web standards pages use headings, unlike old-fashioned sites which often use images or bold text instead, they tend to get better search engine positions.

Finally, sites that are accessible and use web standards rely less on normal images (using the `<img … />` tag) and more on background images, compared to old-fashioned sites. Also, they're much more likely to include ALT text when images are used. Image heavy sites without ALT text tend to do badly in search engines because they can only read text, not images.

Microformats: an SEO technique of the future?

Every web page contains information. Most websites have a contact page, with a phone number, email address and possibly a street address. Others have reviews of products, books or CDs.

Microformats are a way to label certain information, like contact details or reviews, so it can easily be extracted from your web page by a suitable computer program or website.

They're easy to use and, although they're currently very new, they're worth adding to your site because they could prove a useful SEO technique for the future as sites spring up to harvest data stored in microformats. See page 136 for more information.

Don't forget

"Web standards" are a modern approach to building websites, using XHTML, CSS and unobtrusive Javascript, that ensures they work correctly in any modern browser (see page 153).

173

Hot tip

It's early days for microformats, but they could become a great way to increase traffic to your website.

http://kitchen. technorati.com/search/ is a microformats search engine you can add your site to—if you use them.

Blogging & podcasting

Blogs are a fantastic way to make people aware of your product or service. A well written, informative and regularly updated blog is a great way to gain a reputation as an expert in your field.

A blog should help your search engine ranking as you will be producing new content on a regular basis, which naturally contains a variety of keywords that relate to your business.

People are also much more likely to link to a blog than a purely commercial site, which should help increase your link popularity.

If you set up a blog for your business, it's important to stay focused on one topic. If people have come to your site because of your knowledge of photography, they're unlikely to care that you're having trouble selling your car.

Blogs are easy to set up using special blogging software like Wordpress (**wordpress.com**) or Movable Type (**moveabletype.org**). Blogger (**blogger.com**) is a great entry-level blogging tool and is very easy to set up (see page 149). However, you may want something a bit more powerful and flexible for a commercial blog.

What is podcasting?
The word "podcasting" comes from squashing the words "iPod" and "broadcasting" together.

A podcast is similar to a radio show, but, instead of broadcasting over the radio, it is saved as an MP3 audio file. Listeners can subscribe to a podcast using iTunes (**www.itunes. com**) or a similar program, which automatically downloads the latest podcast when it is published.

You can find podcasts using iTunes or through a directory like **www.podcast. net** or **www.jellycast.com**

Like blogging, podcasting is a great way to promote your business and establish yourself as an expert in your field.

All you need to make a podcast is a computer, a microphone and some free audio editing software like Audacity (**http://audacity.sf.net**).

Advertise with Google AdWords

Getting your site to the top of the search engines can be a slow process. There's a lot of work involved and a fair amount of luck.

Wouldn't it be great if there was a way to get people to visit your site without going through all the hassle? Well there is. You can pay Google to promote your site using *Google AdWords*.

1 AdWords ads appear as "sponsored links", either above the main search results or (more often) to the right.

2 The more you bid on AdWords, the higher up the sponsored links you'll come.

Introducing AdWords

When you do a search using Google, you will usually see some links on the right-hand side of the screen. These are *sponsored links* which have been paid for by advertisers.

Just like Google's normal results, sponsored links will match the keywords you searched for. However, with AdWords you get to decide the keywords your ad should show up for yourself.

As well as appearing on Google's search results page, AdWords ads appear on relevant websites and blogs.

How much do they cost?

You pay a certain amount of money every time somebody clicks on one of your ads. The amount you pay can range from a few cents to several dollars. However, the great thing is that you can set the maximum amount you're prepared to pay.

AdWords advertisers bid against each other, so the more you pay, the higher up you'll come in the sponsored results.

Hot tip

The trick with AdWords is to choose keywords where you won't have to pay lots just to appear on the first page.

It would cost you several dollars a visitor to come top for a competitive keyword like "SEO".

However, you might be able to get on the first page of "SEO Chicago" for as little as 5 cents.

The 5 worst SEO mistakes

It's obviously useful knowing how to rank well in search engines, but what are the mistakes you should avoid at all costs?

1 Making your whole site from Flash

Flash is great, in moderation, but search engines struggle to index sites created in it. By all means use Flash on your site, but don't build the whole site in it. Avoid using Flash for your navigation for the same reasons.

2 Using Javascript for your navigation

Google doesn't use Javascript, so if your site navigation relies on it to work, Google won't know your pages exist. Avoid using DHTML drop-down menus if you can, or opt for a search engine friendly alternative, like the web standards *suckerfish drop-downs* technique described at **http://alistapart.com/articles/dropdowns/**

3 Using frames

Frames make it hard for Google to index your site. They also mean that people who *do* find it are likely to be stranded on a page without any navigation. For more information about issues with frames, see page 158.

4 Using tables for layout

Before web standards, the only way to get a web page to look exactly how you wanted was to use data tables to position the content and images. However, tables use lots more code than web standards (using XHTML and CSS), meaning the main content will appear lower down on the page – and therefore less important – to Google.

5 Misusing images

Commercial web pages should look attractive. However, bear in mind that Google is blind, so it can't see the images on your site. If your page is full of images and has no text (and no ALT text), then Google doesn't know what it's about, so it can't index it. Use images sparingly (or use background images instead) and make sure there are at least 50 words of content on each page you want indexed.

4 cheap ways to market your site

Promoting your site can be expensive, but what if you haven't got a large marketing budget? Here are some techniques you can use.

1 **Add yourself to free web directories**
There are hundreds of web directories that allow you to post your details for free. As well as general web directories, there are ones that list sites of a specific type (food websites, carpentry websites) or location. There's a good list of web directories here: **http://info.vilesilencer.com**

2 **Post on message boards**
Message boards are websites (or sections of sites) where people go to chat, usually about a single subject. There are message boards about everything from puppies to politics.

Posting on message boards is a great way to pick up a few extra visitors. Most message boards allow you to add your web address to your signature. **NEVER** post messages advertising your site or service, you'll just annoy people. Instead, join message boards that interest you or relate to your website in some way. Don't be controversial, just be helpful and people will visit your site out of interest.

3 **Write some articles**
A very effective way of getting people to visit your site is to write articles (about something closely related to your site) and then submit them to an article marketing service like **articlemarketer.com, ideamarketers.com** or **ezinearticles.com**. You won't get paid for your article, but you can put a link to your site in your biography. Other sites will be able to publish your article, so you could get dozens or even hundreds of incoming links to your site, boosting its Google ranking and drawing in traffic.

4 **Ask other sites for links**
Link exchanges won't really help your Google ranking (Google's too smart for that), but you will pick up a few extra visitors who click on the link. Ask other sites to put a link to you on their "links page" in exhange for a link to them on yours.

Hot tip

One of the keys to a successful article is a great title. People are more likely to read an article called "5 ways to improve your Google ranking," than "The Google Page Rank algorithm: an in-depth analysis."

Getting 'real world' exposure

With all the coverage search engines, blogs and pay-per-click advertising get, it would be easy to forget that online promotion isn't the *only* way to advertise your website.

Traditional promotion still has its place, whether it's radio slots, magazine and newspaper ads, flyers or public relations.

The bare minimum

Most businesses have some kind of real world presence, whether it's a shop, catalogue or just a customer helpline.

Make sure whenever you make contact with them, you remind your customers about your website. Among other things, you should include your website address on:

- letterheads, invoices and business cards
- receipts and bags
- your answering machine message
- staff uniforms, if appropriate
- the sides of your vans and delivery trucks
- your shop window

Traditional advertising

Before the Internet came along, businesses relied on a wide variety of marketing avenues to bring new business in. There's no reason you can't use traditional methods to promote your website.

The cost will usually be higher than SEO or pay-per-click ads, so it's important to ensure your offline marketing is well targeted. An ad for your snowboard site will probably get a better response in a specialist snowboard magazine than your local newspaper.

Some methods you could consider include:

- word of mouth recommendations
- TV and radio ads
- newspaper and magazine ads
- newspaper and magazine editorial (news stories and reviews)
- direct mail and flyers
- posters and billboards

Promoting your site with email

How many people do you think will buy from your website the very first time they visit it? Not many. In fact, experts believe it usually takes between 5 and 12 visits to your site before an average customer will do business with you.

So, in order to get people to buy from you (or contact you, if that's the goal of your site), you need to get them to come back to it more than once–but how can you do this?

Without encouragement, a few people might bookmark your site, but most will simply leave, never to return.

One great way to get people to return to your site, is to get them to sign up for your email mailing list. Then you can send them regular emails reminding them about your site, as well as telling them about your latest news and special offers.

Offering your visitors the chance to win something, like gift cards, will make them much more likely to sign up to your mailing list.

179

You don't get anything for nothing
If you simply ask people for their email address, a few people might sign up, but you'll get a much better response if you offer your visitors something in return.

For example, you could offer them the chance to win a copy of your latest book or give them the opportunity to download a free white paper called, "10 ways to promote your website."

Sending an effective email
Getting people's email addresses isn't much use if you don't send them an email that encourages them to revisit your site and buy from you or use your service.

You should pay special attention to the way the email's written. Remember, you're trying to sell your site to people, so use the AIDA technique (Attention, Interest, Desire, Action) to grab your readers' attention and make them take action.

Don't overdo the hard sell, though. If you've promised your subscribers an email newsletter, it's important you have some actual news in it, not just a sales pitch.

Looks matter
It's often worth sending an HTML email, rather than a normal, text-based email as the impact is greater. Bear in mind, though, that some people might not be able view the email properly.

Don't forget

See page 50 for more information about writing sales copy using the AIDA technique.

Google.com/analytics allows you to track your visitors in great detail – what's more it's free.

Crazyegg.com is a service that allows you to track which regions of your pages people are clicking on.

It's very useful for seeing how effective your design is, so you can make changes if needed.

Who's visiting your website?

One of the great things with a website is that you can track exactly who's visiting it, what type of computer they use, which pages they've seen and even which country they come from.

Most web hosts provide a basic *web statistics* package free of charge, or you could use a service like Mint (**haveamint.com**) or Google Analytics (**google.com/analytics/**).

Understanding web statistics

You'll often hear people talking about the number of *hits* their website gets. This number usually sounds impressive, but you should treat it with caution.

Your site gets a "hit" every time a file is downloaded. This includes images and css files, which means that when someone visits your homepage they could download dozens of files.

A more useful statistic to look at is the number of *unique visitors* to your site. If you've had 1000 unique visitors it means 1000 potential customers have visited your site.

In Google Analytics, the menu on the left lets you look at different statistics. Some things you might like to look at are:

- daily visitors – how many visitors you've had today
- referring source – which websites sent people your way
- geo location – where in the world your visitors live
- overall keyword conversion – what keywords people are searching for in Google to find your site?
- connection speed – are your visitors using broadband?

How to use this information

Finding out how many visitors you've had from Samoa or the British Virgin Islands may be fun, but the real power of statistics is to help you improve your website and SEO strategy.

If lots of people visit your homepage but leave straight away, you should examine the design to see how to improve it.

If you get 3,000 visitors a day, that's encouraging. However, if your company is called Bill Gates Building Supplies and 99% of your visitors find your site after typing "Bill Gates" into Google, then you've probably only had around 30 genuine visitors – the rest were searching for the founder of Microsoft.

The dark side of SEO

SEO has a bit of a bad name within the web design industry. It's often thought of by web designers as seedy and unethical.

In part, this is down to ignorance and misunderstanding on the part of web designers and developers–but only in part.

Some so-called SEO professionals have used underhand techniques, over the years, to try to trick Google and other search engines into giving their sites an unfairly high ranking.

Google understandably takes any attempts to trick it very seriously. If (or rather when) you're found to have cheated, Google can penalize your site or even ban it altogether.

Black hat and white hat SEO

It's perfectly OK to try to help your site do as well as possible in search engines. The techniques described in this chapter are all fine and you shouldn't be penalized by Google for using them.

Ethical techniques like these are known as *white hat* SEO. By contrast, unethical techniques are known as *black hat* SEO.

Black hat techniques are ones that a reasonable person (and more importantly Google) would consider cheating. Examples of black hat SEO include:

- keyword stuffing–cramming long lists of keywords into your pages without any other content

- invisible text–hiding text from your visitors, but showing it to search engines (e.g. white text on a white background)

- doorway pages–pages that exist for search engines but not visitors (who are automatically redirected to your real site)

If you're unsure if a technique is ethical, ask yourself if you would be happy if you discovered one of your competitors was using the technique. If not, don't use it yourself.

Techniques like these do work–for a while. However, sooner or later Google will realize you're cheating. Then, your site will be penalized and could be banned from Google–forever.

Unless you're only planning to be in business for a few weeks, black hat SEO should be avoided.

And finally...

Introducing the blog...

Learning to design websites is an exciting and fascinating journey. Of course, you're not at the end of that journey yet. However, now you've read this book, you've taken the first step.

To help you on the next step of your journey, I've set up a blog to accompany the book.

I'll be posting articles and tutorials, answering questions from readers, letting you know about useful products and keeping you up to date with the latest developments in web design. Please drop in and check it out.

Go to **http://www.web-design-book.com**

If you've used this book to help you design a website, I'd love to hear from you. There's a showcase section on the blog, where you can post a link to your site and tell everyone about it.

...and podcast

As well as the blog, I've started a podcast to accompany the book. In each episode, I'll be covering a different aspect of web design, keeping you up to date with the latest developments in the profession and answering questions from *In Easy Steps* readers.

Go to **http://www.web-design-book.com/podcast**

What are you waiting for? Get started!

There's no better way to learn web design than to dive right in and start making your first site.

There are some great resources online to teach you all aspects of web design.

Finally, don't forget to check out the other books in the *In Easy Steps* series. There are books on Photoshop, HTML, CSS, Javascript, Dreamweaver – in fact every aspect of web design.

Go to **http://www.ineasysteps.com**

Accessibility
The practice of making websites easy to use for disabled people.

Admin area
A password-protected section of a website, which allows the site owner to update its content.

AdWords
Sponsored advertising on Google. AdWords are pay-per-click, meaning you pay a set rate each time someone clicks on your ad.

AIDA
Attention, Interest, Desire, Action
An approach to writing sales copy.

AJAX
Asynchronous Javascript and XML
A modern way of programming websites, so they behave more like programs on a PC.

API
Application Programming Interface
A way for two computer programs to talk to each other. They allow you to use functions from other websites, like Google Maps or Amazon.

ASP
Active Server Pages
A server-side programming language made by Microsoft and similar to Visual Basic. The latest version is ASP .NET.

Bandwidth
The speed of your Internet connection. Also, the amount of data that can be downloaded from your site per month.

Blog
Short for web log
An easy-to-update personal website. Often used as an online diary.

Broadband
A fast Internet connection.

Browser
A program for looking at websites. Common browsers include Internet Explorer, Firefox, Safari and Opera.

Call to action
An element on a web page instructing visitors to perform a certain action, e.g. a "buy now" button.

Client-side programs
Programs that run on your computer, as opposed to on the server. Client-side programs normally use Javascript.

CMS
Content Management System
A computer program which allows website owners to update their website without needing to know HTML. Usually a server-side program.

CMYK
Cyan, Magenta, Yellow and Black (Key)
The way colors are composed in printed documents, using dots of cyan, magenta, yellow and black ink.

CSS
Cascading Style Sheets
A language used in conjunction with HTML to style web pages: can be used to set fonts and colors as well as to control the layout of web pages.

Database
A way of storing information (data) on a computer.

DHTML
Dynamic HTML
A way of using Javascript and CSS to make elements on web pages move.

Domain name
The name of your website. E.g. **bn.com** or **ineasysteps.com**

DPI
Dots Per Inch
The unit for measuring the resolution of an image. The higher the dpi, the sharper it is. Images on websites are 72dpi, compared to 300dpi for print.

Dreamweaver
A popular web design program.

Ecommerce
Any business done over the Internet, including online shops.

FAQ
Frequently Asked Questions

Firefox
The second most popular web browser. Available on PC and MAC computers.

Flash
A plug-in which allows browsers to display animations.

Forms
Part of a web page that lets users enter information and send it to the server. The information is usually used by a server-side program (written in a language like PHP or ASP).

FTP
File Transfer Protocol
The way files are uploaded from your computer to your web server, using an FTP program.

Gif
Graphics Interchange Format
An image format used on websites. Good for non-photographic images.

Grids
Guidelines used to design a website.

Hosting account
An account with a company which allocates you space on its servers.

Hotspot
A region of a web page that people are more likely to look at than others.

HTML
HyperText Markup Language
The programming language web pages are written in.

Internet
A world-wide network of computers.

Internet Explorer
The most popular web browser. Comes on Windows PCs as standard.

Internet merchant account
A bank account which allows a business to accept online credit card payments.

ISP
Internet Service Provider
The company which provides your Internet connection. e.g. AOL.

Javascript

A programming language which runs in your web browser. Used to make websites more interactive.

Jpeg / jpg

Joint Photographic Experts Group
An image format used on websites. Good for photographic images.

Keywords

Words which people search for in Google and other search engines.

Link

Words or images on a web page which, when clicked, take you to another web page (or part of the same page).

Mashup

An innovative use of an API to create an interesting website.

META tags

Hidden HTML tags which used to be very useful for search engine optimization, but no longer are.

Microformats

A way to mark up information on web pages so it can easily be extracted by computer programs.

Modem

A device to help you connect to the Internet using a phone line. Many people now use faster broadband connections, rather than modems.

Mouseover

A link which changes visually when you move your mouse pointer over it, for example, changing color. Also called an *image rollover*.

MySQL

My Structured Query Language
A popular database, often used with PHP to create dynamic websites.

Page rank

A number allocated to web pages by Google, to help it rank pages. Based on the number of inbound links a page has.

PayPal

A popular way to take payments online, including credit cards.

PDA

Personal Digital Assistant
A handheld computer.

PDF

Portable Document Format
A type of electronic document designed to be easily shared.

Photoshop

A popular graphics program used to design websites.

PHP

Pre-Hypertext Processor
Probably the most popular server-side programming language. Used to create dynamic websites, often in conjunction with a MySQL database.

Plug-in

A small program which extends a web browser's capabilities.

Podcasts

iPod broadcasts
Radio-style shows which are saved as MP3 audio files and automatically downloaded to your computer.

PPC

Pay-per-click

A popular form of online advertising used by Google AdWords (among others). Advertisers pay a set fee every time someone clicks on their ad.

RGB

Red, Green and Blue

The way colors on a computer screen are composed, using dots of red, green and blue light.

ROI

Return on investment

The amount of money you make for every dollar you spend.

RSS

Really Simple Syndication

A way for website owners to let regular visitors know about updates.

SEO

Search Engine Opimization

The art of helping sites do well in Google and other search engines.

Server

A computer which is permanently connected to the Internet and "serves" web pages. Also, the program it runs, allowing it to serve web pages.

Server-side program

A program which runs on a web server. Usually produces HTML and CSS to send to your computer. Server-side programs are written in languages like PHP or ASP.

Sitemap

A plan of a website. Also, a web page with links to the main pages on a site.

Tags

Bits of HTML code. Tags are used to add extra information to text, as well as to add images and other elements to web pages.

URL

Uniform resource locator

The address of a web page. E.g. **www.web-design-book.com/podcast**

USP

Unique Selling Point

A quality which makes a product or service better than its competitors.

Validation

A way to automatically check your HTML code.

Web

A standard way of publishing information on the Internet.

Web standards

A modern approach to building sites.

Wireframes

Working protoypes of a website, which are used for user testing.

XHTML

Extensible HTML

A modern version of HTML, often used with CSS to produce web standards websites.

XML

Extensible Markup Language

A language based on tags. Similar to HTML, but more flexible (and not suitable for websites). Often used to store data instead of a database.

Index